The Politics of Biblical Theology

And where do you look for this hope that you're seekin'?
Where do you look for this lamp that's a burnin'?
Where do you look for this oil well gushin'?
Where do you look for this candle that's blowin'?
Where do you look for the hope that you know is out there somewhere?
And your feet can only walk down two kinds of roads.
Your eyes can only look down two kinds of windows.
Your nose can only smell two kinds of hallways.
You can touch and twist and turn two kinds of doorknobs.
You can either go to the church of your choice,
or to Brooklyn State Hospital.
You find God in the church of your choice.
You find Woody Guthrie in Brooklyn State Hospital.
You know, it's only my opinion.
I may be right or wrong.
You find both at Grand Canyon, at sundown.

—Bob Dylan, "Last Thoughts on Woody Guthrie"

• *Studies in American Biblical Hermeneutics 10* •

The Politics of Biblical Theology

A Postmodern Reading

by
David Penchansky

MERCER

ISBN 0-86554-462-X   MUP/P1 15

The Politics of Biblical Theology.
A Postmodern Reading.
Copyright ©1995
Mercer University Press, Macon, Georgia 31210-3960 USA
All rights reserved
Printed in the United States of America

The paper used in this publication meets
the minimum requirements of American National Standard
for Information Sciences—Permanence of Paper
for Printed Library Materials, ANSI Z39.48-1984.

Library of Congress Cataloging-in-Publication Data

Penchansky, David, 1951–   .
The politics of biblical theology :
A postmodern reading /
by David Penchansky.
ix+109 pp. 6x9" (15x23 cm.).
(Studies in American biblical hermeneutics : 10).
Includes bibliographical references and indexes.
ISBN 0-86554-462-X (pbk.; alkaline paper).
1. Bible—Theology—Study and teaching—History—20th century.
2. Bible—Criticism, interpretation, etc.—History—20th century.
3. Postmodernism—Religious aspects—Christianity.
I. Title. II. Series.
BS543.P44   1995
230—dc20   95-5759
                                              CIP

Contents

Editor's Preface

In *The Politics of Biblical Theology*, David Penchansky discusses the willful aspect of the interpretive process. In language born in the insights of postmodernism, he instructs us about the way we force a voice upon the biblical text that affirms our most deeply held convictions, many of which are political in nature. This book will not be easy reading for those who hold that meaning flows without cumbrance from text to reader. The view that such interpretive choices necessarily take place in the context of community and culture conforms to a common assumption of contributors to this series. The key insight here is that the reader of the biblical text participates in the production of its meaning. In fact, this insight is the generative force behind all the books of this series. Penchansky's work is peppered with postmodern terms that come with the acknowledgment of the subjective, political dimension of academic thought: "ideology," "deconstruction," "binary opposition," and the like. Such words confirm Penchansky's own brand of hermeneutical suspicion (somewhat reminiscent of Ricoeur) that searches surface fissures and cracks for indications of a subterranean world of unverifiable assumptions and presuppositions that frequently go unattended on the surface level of the academic retelling of the biblical text. It is precisely those fissures and cracks that Penchansky addresses with provocative vitality and sensitivity. Whether the reader agrees or disagrees, the reader can hardly deny the singleness of purpose from which this book springs.

The conceptual center of Penchansky's work is an analysis of the Biblical Theology Movement that was a matter of substantial interest in the academic study of the Bible at the midpoint of the twentieth century. Penchansky probes both the major apologists of this movement, with special reference to the works of Thorlief Boman and G. Ernest Wright, as well as those associated with its subsequent fall from academic grace. This fall was facilitated by such influential religious scholars as James Barr and Langdon Gilkey. Penchansky shows that while Christian hegemony may have formed the inner political cores of the Biblical Theology Movement itself, equally subjective and self-serving political considerations motivated its detractors as well. It seems the loss of Christian hegemony within scholarly discourse of the Bible has *not* resulted in the loss of such self-interest! In arguing for the heavy hand of political choice in the dynamic of biblical interpretation, Penchansky intends to probe the "mind" of the academic study of the Bible in our cultural context. The Biblical Theology Movement, and the attack upon it, is an academic parable that illustrates forces that continue to be at work in the academy. The fact that the movement by and large seems to have succumbed to those forces is not in and of itself an indictment in absolute terms of the insights that it brought to the interpretive process.

Throughout this work Penchansky illustrates the dictum that no interpretation is value free. He argues that in recent years we have become ever more conscious in the American interpretive context of a de-centered Bible. The further question that lies before us is where does this realization take us? To despair at our irreducible subjectivity? No, certainly such pessimism does not represent the tenor of Penchansky's argument. While this book is an *affirmation* of the impossibility of a definitive reading of the biblical text, this relativity is the open door through which we may self-consciously reclaim such values as self-limitation, responsibility, and imagination in the act of reading. We might say that such categories of human experience are "gifts" that we bring to the biblical text because they have the potential of enlarging and deepening the narrow intentionality of the human authors imbedded within it. Penchansky concludes his study by suggesting something of the potential of this more honest and self-conscious way of reading the Bible.

Deconstructive categories of thought have proven to be quite contentious in the American academy in the late twentieth century. And, as might be expected, the controversies that mark philosophic and literary-critical discourse have spilled over into the theological community as well. In many ways, the jury is still out in terms of the ultimate contribution this approach will make with regard to biblical study: whether or not, on balance, it will prove to be a constructive liberating force. The Studies in American Biblical Hermeneutics series is not wedded to any one particular approach to the study of the Bible and the way that our cultural experience influences our understanding of it. Yet it is committed to the idea that strong arguments about the forces that clandestinely shape the interpretive process within our cultural context need to be clearly set forth if we are to sift the wheat from the tares and recapture a Bible that moves and convicts us as a society. To that end, I believe David Penchansky has made a solid contriburtion with this very provocative book.

Ecumenical Theological Seminary   *Charles Mabee*
Detroit

Chapter 1

Introduction to the Field and to the Methodology

We should not restrict meaning to the cognitive core that lies at the heart of a knowable object; rather, we should allow it to reestablish its flux at the limit of words and things.
—Michel Foucault, *Language, Counter-Memory, Practice* (174)

I speak of certain biblical critics, and not about the Bible. But frequently biblical critics mimic or reproduce issues already fashioned within the biblical material. I speak of a conflict which takes place over texts, and so I shall begin with a retelling of a biblical conflict.

And the spirit of YHWH came mightily upon David from that day forward. . . . And the Spirit of YHWH departed from Saul, and an evil spirit from YHWH began to torment him. (1 Sam 16:13b-14)

This biblical text concerns two individuals, the young man David, destined to be king, and the older man King Saul. What takes place is not an event strictly speaking, nothing anyone watching would be able to see. But these two short verses provide the narrative crux around which hinges the story of David's rise to power.

First, we have a relationship of inequality. Saul is a great king living in an urban center, while David is young, and from the country. Subsequently, Saul becomes David's sponsor, which further establishes the hierarchy between the two. The story recounts the reversal of this hierarchy. Before the story ends, Saul and most of his family are dead while David becomes high king over all Israel.

God brings about the exchange of power, not directly, but through the unequal exchange of mediating forces. One force, called "the spirit of YHWH," usually associated with divinely appointed leadership, is taken from one, Saul, and given to another, David.

Here the narrator breaks the simple symmetry of the story. It appears upon first glance to be a simple rise and fall: Saul is up, and then he is down. David is down, and then he is up. Saul has the holy Spirit, and then he does not. David does not have the holy Spirit, and then he does.

An evil spirit is given to Saul to torment him. To make the symmetry complete, the evil spirit would have had to come from David, but it has not been taken from David. The evil spirit comes directly from YHWH. YHWH sends the evil spirit.

Although the association of evil spirits with deity might not have appeared as strange in ancient Israel as it does to us today, it must still have sent a chill. And we dislike YHWH's actions here for their sheer gratuitousness. Why send an evil spirit to torment Saul?

Did YHWH punish Saul for his sins?

Did YHWH seek to undermine Saul so as to facilitate David's rise to power?

Is this simply a spiritual explanation of Saul's very understandable decline into depression and paranoia, as he felt the power of office gradually slip from his hands?

In what precedes this text, we may learn that Saul was no devil. From what follows, we learn that David was no angel. But that is the way things frequently go. The ones who lose power come to appear as demons, while the ones who ascend to dominance bask in the unalloyed glow of divine approval.

This book explores a more contemporary example of this age-old story of rise and fall, fall and rise. In this contemporary story too, there is the gratuitous evil spirit, adding insult, visited upon the loser.

Saul has killed his thousands and David his ten thousands.

(1 Sam 18:7)

Here too we have a seemingly simple phrase that underscores the difference between the two men, a tenfold difference. The act of ending one thousand lives (certainly here meant figuratively) is unimaginably cruel and barbaric. But David is ten times as horrible, ten times more the mass murderer than his patron.

Clearly the author means to demonstrate David's superiority as a warrior, that the charismatic mantle has fallen upon him.

But they are the same! Is it so much worse (or better) to kill one thousand or ten thousand? The Talmud claims that

> Whoever kills one life in Israel, it is as if he killed the whole world; whoever saves a life in Israel, it is as if he saved the whole world.   (Mishnah *Sanhedrin* 4:5; Talmud *Baba Batra* 11a;
> Maimonides *Laws of Murder* 1:16)

And so it is with our story. What makes our protagonists different, the exchanges of influence and dominance that takes place, is also that which makes them the same.

• Staking Out the Field •

> When power is at issue, "truth" and "untruth" are your instruments.   (F. G. Baily, *The Prevalence of Deceit*, 46)

The First Part—The Field of Study

> If one is always bound by one's perspective, one can at least deliberately reverse perspectives as often as possible in the process undoing opposed perspectives, showing that the two terms of an opposition are merely accomplices of each other.
> (Jacques Derrida, *On Grammatology*, xxviii)

Let me first set out the boundaries of the material I will examine, for such boundaries can be expanded infinitely if they are not rather arbitrarily defined. I am examining a particular moment in the history of biblical criticism that encompasses the years of the 1940s, the 1950s, and part of the 1960s. During this time period (as I will analyze later in this work) the so-called Biblical Theology

Movement rose to prominence, and also during these two decades or so, certain individual scholars exposed the weaknesses of the Biblical Theology Movement and drove its proponents from the public arena in shame. It was a power play, an effort to drive out the ruling priests of the academic world.

I will examine the work of the following individuals who wrote during this period and who played their part in shaping the discourse: Thorlief Boman, the Norwegian scholar who wrote in German the classic work *Das hebräische Denken im Vergleich mit dem Griechischen* (2nd ed. 1954), translated into English as *Hebrew Thought Compared with Greek* (1960); and North American Scholar G. Ernest Wright who wrote the influential best seller *God Who Acts* (1952).

Boman's book is a careful analysis of the dramatic differences between the ways the Hebrews and the Greeks thought, the ways they conceived reality, and how these differences were expressed through the fine points of their language. That is, one could find in the differences between Greek and Hebrew grammar all of their differences in theology. Boman was relatively cautious in the conclusions he drew from this claim, whereas many who built on Boman expanded his claims so far as to assert that the New Testament, in contrast to the Old, was purely a Greek invention and thereby deficient.

Wright's thesis, although related to Boman's, explains the contrast between Hebrew and Greek thought forms and between the Old and New Testaments using different terminology and categories. It is likely Wright was not dependent upon Boman for his ideas. Wright's thesis was that God revealed Godself through mighty historical acts, dramatic miracles performed in the presence of the Israelites and on their behalf. This distinctive way in which God worked with Israel absolutely distinguished them from other ancient religions of the time. These other ancient Near Eastern religions did not work with history as such but rather with the repeated cycles of nature; thus these other religions were different from that of the Israelites, even supposedly inferior. Monotheism, the cultic law, Israelite ethics and social justice, and many other features were all thought to stem from this crucial difference.

Therefore in my book Boman and Wright will serve as representatives of a larger group of scholars who seemed to share their basic assumptions.

Finally, I will examine the band of young scholars who were united, as far as I can tell, only by their absolute hatred of and disappointment in the promise of the Biblical Theology Movement, James Barr in particular, whose seminal work *The Semantics of Biblical Language* (1961), along with a few other works, shocked the biblical scholarly community with a powerful and cogent argument against practically everything the Biblical Theology Movement stood for, declaring that the emperor was completely unclothed. The faults of the Biblical Theology Movement were displayed for all to see; the public ridicule was devastating.

In the same year, but from a different quarter, there came a scathing attack on the assumptions of Wright's *God Who Acts*. Langdon Gilkey's "Cosmology, Ontology, and the Travail of Biblical Language" characterized Wright's efforts as unscientific and biased, a desperate and unsuccessful attempt on Wright's part to preserve both the miraculous element of the biblical account while at the same time claiming to draw only upon the archaeological and literary evidence. Gilkey demonstrates that the attempt to manifest the superiority of the Israelite religion on the basis of the historical nature of its revelation, founders badly upon the rocks of close examination.

I have often wondered why—if Barr's and Gilkey's critique was so devastating—that ten years later another major scholar, Brevard Childs, saw fit to invade the same presumably conquered territory. I had always sensed that to some extent Childs was beating a dead horse, but in fact his interests were significantly different from Barr's and Gilkey's. There are however reasons why each scholar makes a distinctive contribution. Although Barr, Gilkey, and Childs all occupied roughly the same scholarly space, they speak to very different audiences. Barr and Childs are mainstream biblical theologians, while Gilkey's interest ran more towards *systematic* theology, although with a strong interest in biblical hermeneutics.

In any case, Childs and Gilkey produced equally devastating critiques of the Biblical Theology Movement in its various parts, while Barr attacked the Movement's assumption that a distinctive Israelite theology could be gleaned from Hebrew grammar. Barr's was mainly a deconstructive theology: he attacked an inadequate and ill-founded methodology, but did not try to offer anything in its place, save clear thinking and common sense.

Childs however is avid in his efforts at reconstruction. Child's ambition can be traced back to his *Biblical Theology in Crisis* (1970), is which the germ of his idea is represented. Childs posits in the last chapter a new way to approach biblical texts, *canonically* instead of historically. Thereby, Childs claims to be able to overcome the problems that destroyed the Biblical Theology Movement.

The issue for these three—Barr, Gilkey, and Childs—was the claim of transcendence. Childs, in contrast to Gilkey and Barr, claims he can preserve the transcendence of a text by reading the Bible canonically. Childs feels he has found the answer that the Biblical Theology Movement lacked. He wants nothing less than to inherit the scepter of authority that previously belonged to Boman, Wright, and their confreres. Barr and Gilkey question the possibility of traditional formulations of transcendence.

So the domain of this study, here briefly surveyed, are the selected works of Boman, Wright, Barr, Gilkey, and Childs. And although it is relatively easy to place the Biblical Theology Movement and the trio of Barr, Gilkey, and Childs in opposition to each other, I will here claim that all are similar expressions of a single period in the history of contemporary intellectual life, that of "High Modernism." And "High Modernism," in turn, must be situated with regard to the modern phenomenon known as "Postmodernism."

• The Interaction of Postmodernism and Biblical Criticism •

I define *postmodern* as incredulity towards metanarratives.
(Lyotard, "Postmodern Tradition")

• Four Tendencies in Postmodernism •

The definition of postmodernism is very slippery, and has little coherence. The schema of the section title above is rather arbitrary. There are any number of postmodern features that others have argued are equally important, or perhaps more important.[1] But these

---

[1]Some important features of postmodernism that I do not cover in this chapter are:

(1) Issues of periodization, in which critics examine the actual process by which disorganized data of history are categorized according to historical "periods," and how such periodization affects the interpretation of ancient texts.

(2) The decentered subject as a new form of modernism's alienated loner, the notion that there as no single unified figure that might be called "author" or "character," but rather complex notions of "implied" authors and readers, "idealized" authors and readers.

(3) There is no single ruling metaphor or dominant metanarrative in postmodernism. Instead many different metaphors clash in a central field, each vying for dominance.

(4) The breakdown in postmodernism between the elite and the common, high culture vs. low culture, etc.

(5) Dissonance as a key interpretive feature (see my *Betrayal of God* 1990).

(6) Postmodernism is self-referential in two ways: (a) postmodern critics attend to the processes by which they reach interpretation; and (b) postmodern critics deconstruct their own interpretations.

(7) Postmodernism attacks the accepted canon of a given culture.

(8) Postmodernism tends to emphasize the spatial over the temporal, although Jameson argues that this is negative and should not be accepted.

four "keys" have been especially helpful for me when I interpret scripture and when I reflect upon the processes of interpretation.

1. *Contradictions.* The definitions of the two terms *modernism* and *postmodernism* are complex and sometimes self-contradictory. It is a feature of postmodern thought that contradictions inhere at the very heart of things, so one would expect that the definition of its two terms would be fraught with contradictions. Modernism and postmodernism are terms defined by people who understand themselves in some sense as postmodernists, even if they are very conflicted about it, like for example Fredric Jameson. Jameson's complex and angst-ridden book *Postmodernism, or the Cultural Logic of Late Capitalism* (1991) alternates with no warning between, on the one hand, blanket condemnations of the excesses and self-absorption of postmodernism, with, on the other, a blatant identification with its precepts. He oscillates between one position railing at postmodernism for its lack of a utopia, to another position in which he suggests some ways that utopia might be incorporated within the postmodern system/antisystem.

A cartoon I saw expresses the tension rather nicely. The cartoon consisted of two panels. In the first, a man with a sick and unhappy expression declares, "Everything sucks." In the next panel, the same man, here depicted as happy and animated, states joyfully, "Everything sucks." Above the first panel it says "Modernism," and over the second "Postmodernism." Modernism anguished over the moral dilemmas and contradictions inherent in their system. This was the angst that the modern hero always felt,

---

(9) Postmodernism tends to be attracted to expressions of technology and media.

(10) Postmodernism uses Reader Response Criticism and Narrative Criticism, although without the stable text that reader-response critics usually presume.

(11) Postmodernism is self-reflective and thereby deconstructs the self of the interpreter.

(12) The method and style of the interpreter, as well as the angst of the interpreter, frequently reflects the style and the angst of the text being interpreted.

the difficulty in acting, or in justifying any action. This is Camus's existential indecision, Satre's nausea. Postmodernism revels and exults in this same tension.

The following are some implications that come from examining texts and the ideologies that support them when they are understood as fraught with contradiction. This is how looking for these contradictions affect my processes of interpretation.

a. I look for contradictions on the surface of the text. These contradictions are often the remains of an ideological struggle that took place during the transmission of this material.

b. Each system, whether a religious system such as the one represented by the Deuteronomist, or an intellectual system such as Marxism, has contradictions at the very heart of its expression. Often by uncovering the contradictions one can neutralize the ideological effect of that system upon the society. But when we expose contradictions in *other* systems, we imply that a good and pure system should have no contradictions, internal conflicts, or mixed definitions. But *every* system contains its own contradictions, and exposing these conflicts does not necessarily invalidate the system.

c. In postmodernism, contradictions are not seen as a problem, but rather as an occasion for creativity.

So I will be examining the contradictions that were exposed in the thinking and conclusions of the Biblical Theology Movement, and will reflect on why the movement was so quickly neutralized by the exposure of these contradictions. I will also be examining the contradictions within the systems of the three who oppose the Biblical Theology Movement. And in doing this examination I will also be exposing my own contradictions.

2. *The Absence of a Center.*

> Turning and turning in the widening gyre
> The falcon cannot hear the falconer;
> Things fall apart; the centre cannot hold;
> Mere anarchy is loosed upon the world, . . .
> (William Butler Yeats, "The Second Coming")

Yeats describes the postmodern moment, a moment wherein the center cannot hold. But Yeats looked upon the ever-weakening circles of the falcon with a bit of terror—he did, after all, describe the second coming as a "rough beast . . . [that] slouches towards Bethlehem to be born." In the postmodern, the process (started in the modern era, recorded by Yeats) is nearly complete. There is no center. There is no up or down. Everything is disoriented, with no possibility of reorientation. A good example of this de-orientation may be found in the *Star Trek* saga. The original episodes of *Star Trek* are high modernist, completely unconscious of how culturally determined (North American, male, and white) they were. "Star Trek: The Next Generation" was aware of this, and sought to deliberately challenge the cultural assumptions of White, North American, male ideology.

But it was not until the very last episode, in a battle between the *Enterprise* and some Klingon warships, that the battling ships were depicted *not on the same two-dimensional plane*. As far as I know, that was the first time in any science fiction that all the participants did not stay on the same plane. It was very disorienting, because there was no up or down. This was the most important event in the entire series, and can be placed on a direct line back to Copernicus declaring that the earth was not the center of the solar system.

This observation impinges directly on the notion that one may find a center, or *mitte* in the Israelite corpus, a ruling metaphor by which the whole is governed. Eichrodt suggested "Covenant" as the *mitte*, but what could he do with the early wisdom literature, which never mentioned the covenant? Others have suggested "Creation," or even "God," but there are problems with each of them. Instead, in this postmodern trope, one must affirm that there are many competing centers.

Also, there can be no center to methodology, the means by which we choose to interpret the Bible. No one method is the "center" from which all the various methods radiate. Lately it has become popular to claim an "eclectic" method, by means of which one attends to all the stages in the process of the writing and transmission of Israelite scripture, attending to the world of the author, the world of the text, and the world of the reader, and thus covering everything important. This is nonsense. Every practitioner of "eclectic" interpretation will elevate a particular focus, and it will not be eclectic. Even the division into three spheres is highly suspect. So although there is not only one method, it seems inevitable that one must choose a method, or a particular cluster of methods, and we must have good reasons for choosing. And our reasons for choosing one method over another are probably always political.

3. *All Readings Are Political.* Readings of texts must always come to grips with the highly political agenda of any literary work, as well as the political agendas of those who read such works.

This means that the various religious transformations that took place in ancient Israel, and the various individuals and groups that participated, in fact had political agendas, particular individuals and factions that they wanted in power, and others that they did not. The literature was written to achieve those ends. It is relatively easy to determine this political overtone in texts like the succession narrative (the story of how King David came to power). Other passages of the Hebrew Bible are more difficult to read politically, where the politics is expressly concealed, as in the Psalms or perhaps in the Book of Job (see Penchansky 1989). Of course, if one moves into this area of ideological criticism (see my "Up for Grabs," Penchansky 1992), one must also politically deconstruct one's own ideological interest.

This does not necessarily mean declaring up front what one's racial, national, gender, and political affiliations are. The politics that count are usually the most concealed. These politics are embedded into the very fabric of one's work, which is often different from one's stated political affiliations.

This brings us to the second observation regarding the interested political nature of a text from the perspective of the postmodern. The first was that the texts themselves were motivated politically. The second observation is that all current readings of ancient texts have a concealed political agenda. In this book, that will come out when we observe that the Biblical Theology Movement was engaged in political activity that expressed itself in the following ways.

a. within the academic guild itself, the Biblical Theology Movement displaced rather successfully the strict historical critics who had previously dominated the field. Then, through various publications (this is the aspect I am examining) they maintained and expanded their ownership of this academic space, repelling all challengers. To this day, the influence of the Biblical Theology Movement on so many unexamined assumptions is phenomenal. Examples will follow in subsequent chapters.

b. The methodological view of the Biblical Theology Movement tended to look upon the ruling tradents (tradition bearers) within the Israelite political/religious/literary system as most important. These ruling tradents would be the ones to support the status quo both in economic and political spheres. There exists a symbiotic relationship between those who have the power to preserve a particular reading and those who actually do the editing, whether priests, prophets, or sages. It is always in the best interests of an author who wants a writing disseminated or published, to placate or at least deceive those who have the authority to suppress one's writing if they are not pleased. So, by default, the Biblical Theology Movement tended to elevate the most conservative members of the Israelite establishment. This is particularly true of the "New Critics" (whom I associate with the Biblical Theology Movement: see below) and the canon critics, who claim attention only for the "final form of the text" and its reception, privileging the very individuals who were most aggressively and successfully hegemonistic. These ruling tradents suppress minority voices who might represent alternative theological understandings.

c. In a larger intellectual sense, the Biblical Theology Movement was responding to and rejecting the liberalism and social engineering of the previous generation in their own time.

Further, we may identify the political battles of those who oppose the Biblical Theology Movement. This will be a subject of chapter four.

4. *Opposition to Bifurcation.* The postmodern critic opposes the division of everything into pairs, the *bifurcation* of reality. There are a number of ways that people understand difficult concepts in terms of two opposing positions. Certainly we have seen our share of threefold (as in author-text-reader) and fourfold divisions (such as Gramsci's square), but the binary is used most widely. This is

true in both modernism and postmodernism. The difference is that in postmodernism the bifurcations are recognized as having no ontological reality, and therefore effort is always made to transcend the polar categories, or failing that, to create new and temporary ones that keep breaking down and reforming themselves. An exploration of a few of these bifurcations should illuminate my point.

a. *Essence and appearance*—also known as "ideology and false consciousness." This is a further elaboration of a more primitive bifurcation, perhaps the first: inside and outside. In an intellectual system, essence is usually identified as that which is superior because it is prior, more substantial, and more permanent. The appearance of things is the shell that must be cracked off before you can find out what is really important. "Beauty is only skin deep." "Don't judge a book by its cover." "It's what's inside that counts." We speak of something that is "shallow, lacking depth" in the most negative sense, particularly when we are speaking of people.

b. The existential model of *authenticity and inauthenticity*. Bultmann, for example, building upon the insights of Schliermacher, insisted that all humans had a basic need for an authentic life, one where the decisions made render life meaningful and autonomous. Of course, the existentialist philosophers felt that contemporary society was fundamentally inauthentic, and had to be overcome through some desperate act of resistance and freedom.

c. *Alienation and liberation*. These terms clearly come from a Marxist model. In the standard vulgar interpretation, alienation is the bad thing imposed upon the innocent proletariat by the capitalists. So, according to this bifurcation, societies can be divided into those that are alienating and those that are liberating, and texts also are forced to take sides. Of course, under the influence of Freud and his followers, Marxists began to see a more psychological aspect of this alienation.

d. In the Structuralist mode, *signifier and signified*. Structuralists use these terms. They have divided the world of discourse, language, and text into these two master categories, signifier and signified. The deliberate presence of the word "sign" in both of these words brings us to the center of structuralism. A "sign" is usually understood to stand in front of "the thing itself," and points back-wards to something that cannot be approached directly, but only through mediation. But the structuralists see things differently. For them, language (the signifier) points to a signified that is not out-side of language, but just a deeper expression of language.

All of these bifurcations, so essential for the ongoing process of thought and evaluation, melt away in the postmodern impulse.

But most prominent in our own study will be the bifurcations essential to so much of recent biblical criticism, bifurcations dividing the Israelite and the pagan, for instance, or between the Hebraic and the Greek. But there are many other bifurcations strongly in operation in the field of biblical criticism. They will be dealt with in subsequent chapters. One of the most exciting features of a postmodern methodology of interpretation, in my opinion, is this willingness to challenge widely accepted polarities, thus seeing things in ever-shifting new configurations.

In summary, in a research project, there are two variables mostly under the control of the researcher. They are the establish-ment of the field of study, which in my case is the Biblical Theol-ogy Movement and early responses to it, and the establishment of method. As I explained, my method will be gleaned from four key features of postmodern thought:

(1) Seeing each text as containing key contradictions, which con-tradictions are a means to access the ideological conflict which is at the heart of textual productions and transmission.

(2) The absence of a center: there is never one key to a text, whether a thematic key to a text or a single methodological key, that will yield all the meaning of the text.

(3) Seeing each text as a site of political and ideological conflict, which means in this case a careful examination of the hidden political assumptions that motivated the theoreticians of the Bibli-cal Theology Movement and the political motives of those who opposed them. Politics, in this case, can refer to very narrow aca-demic politics (who defines the agenda of the Society of Biblical Literature? for instance) or the widest of national and international circumstances.

(4) A strong suspicion against bifurcation, which is the habit of dividing key clusters of intellectual data into polar categories or pairs of contraries. My method suggests that such polarities should be broken down and forced to reconfigure in less accustomed ways.

It now remains for us, in subsequent chapters, to examine these various figures delineated here using the method I have set out. In chapter 2 I will examine the thinking of Thorlief Boman. Chapter 3 approaches the writings of G. Ernest Wright. These are my two representatives who will stand for the whole of the Biblical Theology Movement. Chapter 4 represents my summary of how Barr, Childs, and Gilkey attack the Biblical Theology Movement. In chapter 5 I seek to establish how these issues, located in the past, impinge on contemporary considerations in the field of biblical criticism.

In all, I have in mind to demonstrate how a postmodern methodology might suggest new and fruitful avenues by which to approach the Bible, and to understand the dynamics of how others have approached the Hebrew Scripture.

Chapter 2

Thorlief Boman, Lost and Forgotten

We make the choices we make ultimately on pragmatic, not theoretical grounds. The choices we make as we read about how we read have consequences, and it is those consequences we should become more reflective about.
    —Reed Way Dasenbrock, "Taking It Personally" (276)

There is no escape from the insight which modernity most feared: there is no innocent tradition (including modernity), no innocent classic (including the Scriptures), and no innocent reading (including this one).   —David Tracy, *Dialogue with the Other* (5-6)

• The Politics of *Hebrew Thought Compared with Greek* •

In 1960 Norwegian scholar Thorlief Boman released his book *Hebrew Thought Compared with Greek* in English translation, six years after its publication in German and, curiously, also after two editions had been released in Japanese. Almost simultaneously, James Barr's *Semantics of Biblical Language* (1961) came out. Barr devoted two of his chapters to refuting Boman's thesis (from the German edition). Boman's influence, which had been considerable, was neutralized.

Why should we care about this rather confined scholarly interchange from a previous era? I contend that Boman's ideas need to be reexamined in the light of current developments in biblical studies. Because the roots of the present situation can be found in that prior historical moment and because there are great similarities between that time and our own, we can gain much insight from an examination of Boman and Barr. Since Boman has been virtually forgotten, I will begin by laying out his thesis in as objective a fashion as I can manage. Since Boman's argument depends somewhat on linguistic theory, I will then survey the relevant data, both from James Barr and from non-biblical linguistic theory. Finally, I will begin to examine the relevance of the contemporary scene in the light of this historical moment.

• Boman Found and Remembered •

Boman's thesis is deceptively simple. As his title suggests, he aims to compare the thinking of two disparate cultures, the Hebrew and the Greek. He examines them on the basis of their similarities and their differences.

He assumes that Greek thought is not only more familiar to his audience than Hebrew, but that in fact our culture is structured along Greek lines. Scholars who were his contemporaries had for the most part disparaged the Hebrew as primitive and less evolved than the Greek. Boman argues that rather than being less evolved, the Hebrew way of perceiving the world has its own strength and integrity.

The sense of how Boman (and many others, Pedersen and Herder, for instance) perceived the differences between these worldviews can best be demonstrated from a survey of the ways he draws the contrast: Greek thinking is clear, logical, whereas Hebrew is psychological, based on a subjective understanding. Greek stresses appearances and description; Hebrew, function and properties. Beauty in the Greek system uses form and configuration; the Hebrews base theirs on gracious movement through space. Greeks are concerned with aesthetics; the Hebrews, with function.

Time in the Greek system is based on the sun, and is perceived in a linear manner, separated into past, present, and future, and divided on a line. Hebrew time uses the moon, and relates time to human experience, as in bedtime or mealtime.

Other contrasts I will here briefly mention. In Greek thought, God is transcendent and immanent; in Hebrew, God is eternal and temporal. In Greek objects are known; in Hebrew the subject acts. Greeks excel in science and philosophy; the Hebrews, in religion and morals. The Greek ideal is peaceful and moderate; the Hebrew is passionate. Greeks argue on the basis of the proposition or philosophical proof, whereas the Hebrews argue through parable, repetition, parallelism, and narrative.

There were others at the same time as Boman who articulated similar ideas. Among them are the Scandinavians (Boman, Pedersen, Engnell, and Mowinckel), Herder (*The Spirit of Hebrew Poetry*), and others. They claimed there was a unique *Geist* to the Hebrew culture that was fundamentally different from the *Geist* of the modern era, which was identified as Grecian, which usually meant Platonic. Boman had high regard for Plato, but felt antipathy for Aristotle whom he considered the bane of the Catholic Church. Others regarded Aristotle as simply a continuation of the same Grecian ideas, when compared to the Hebraic.

There were different ways to regard that Hebrew *Geist*. Some, such as Pedersen and Mowinckel, studied it and did not openly theorize as to its relation to any other way of thinking. Others, perhaps for reasons of clarification, but more likely for expressly polemical reasons, highlighted the distinctiveness of the Hebrew *Geist* by explicitly contrasting it with the Greek *Geist*. Boman best exemplifies this approach.

In the process of contrasting the Hebrew with the Greek, Boman assumes a number of things:

(1) That individual cultures did indeed have a distinct *Geist*, that is, characteristic features that distinguish one culture from another.

(2) That these different cultures can be compared. Various features, though not related historically, can make features in other cultures clearer. For instance, pre-Hellenistic Israelite culture had little contact with Platonic Greek, but features characteristic of one may be compared with features characteristic of the other.

(3) That the basis of comparison would be the languages: that is, embedded in each specific language is a kind of genetic code

that holds all of the features of the culture associated with that language. Conversely, one can substantively analyze a vanished culture by examining the grammatical and semantic features of its language; that is, languages get to the very heart in revealing the thought processes of a culture.

(5) Boman tended to privilege the Hebrew *Geist*. This tendency is much clearer in Boman's followers in the Biblical Theology Movement, who claimed not only that the Hebrew *Geist* had been hidden and must be uncovered, but that it was qualitatively much superior.

(6) There was an implied societal critique in the claiming of an (imaginatively constructed) *Geist* for ancient Israel that directly opposed what was seen as the dominant angle of vision of Western culture. The Biblical Theology Movement, under Boman's influence, claimed that modern Western culture embraces Greek intellectual concepts to their detriment.

The antithesis between Hebrew and Greek thought has been a fantastically influential and rhetorically powerful way of understanding the Hebrew Bible, and its influence is felt on all levels of biblical studies. This notion appears frequently within the world of academic biblical studies as well as in sermons and homilies. Through an informal survey I have noted that many biblical scholars began their studies with some similar understanding, and many who would argue against such ideas theoretically still use these same ideas when teaching classes. I must admit I find myself among that number.

But what of the evidence? On what basis does Boman make the claim that Hebrews think this way, or that Greeks think differently? For Boman, Hebrew thought is reflected in their *language*. For Boman, Hebrew—particularly the grammar, the way the words are related, the way the verbs function—exactly reflects this Hebrew mindset.

So, for instance, many have noted the significantly verbal nature of the Hebrew language. Those with a more sophisticated background in Hebrew linguistics will doubtless seek to nuance this observation, but it works into most of our perceptions of

Hebrew speech and writing. At the very least, so many words in Hebrew are verbs or are derived from verbal roots.

It is a short step from this observation, seemingly scientific and objective, to see reflected therein the Hebrew predilection for movement and for function over form and physical appearance. The most theologically revealing and significant words in Hebrew stand for verbal ideas, actions, not some immutable Platonic ideals. *Dabar*, for example, the Hebrew word that refers to "word, matter or thing," is likely derived from its verbal form, referring to the act of speech.

It is in the nature of the grammatical and semantic features of Hebrew that Boman sees reflected an identifiable Hebrew *Geist* or spirit. He then constructs a picture of the nature of the Hebrew mindset which he uses to determine the meaning of various biblical texts.

In 1961, James Barr wrote *The Semantics of Biblical Language* ostensibly to examine and critique certain linguistic arguments used by biblical scholars, but he also shamed and ridiculed those scholars, and destroyed their influence. Boman became the chief target for Barr's critical pen, probably because of Boman's growing influence in Britain and the United States. Earlier reviewers of Boman's work, in both its German and English editions, though generally enthusiastic, always expressed some reservations regarding the scope and far-reaching nature of Boman's claims. No review was so thorough or so effective as that of James Barr. Here we may note in Boman's project the following weaknesses:[1]

(1) Boman was not conversant with a number of important modern developments in the field of linguistics (see below).

(2) Boman's arbitrary determination that Greek was to be identified almost exclusively with Plato is indefensible and does no justice to the development of the Greek culture, which in addition to

---

[1]Although I am using some criticisms from James Barr, this discussion does not represent a systematic analysis of Barr's position, which will be examined in the fourth chapter.

Aristotle includes many other philosophical positions and schools of thought.

(3) Boman is without embarrassment trying to demonstrate the sublimity of the Bible, its reliability, and the superiority of Christianity over other world religions, ancient and modern. Such theological advocacy finds considerably less sympathy in the current era.

(4) Boman disparages what he calls primitive religious impulses such as divination, an unpredictable God, and animism, and he refuses to see them as present in Israelite thought, against overwhelming evidence to the contrary. (Gunkel, for example, uncovered primitive beliefs and practices in the biblical text, such as magic, divination, and the demonic behavior of YHWH.) Boman argues that "the singular value of Israelite thinking is misconstrued by a majority of scholars and mistaken for primitive thinking as though it were prelogical" (Boman 1960, 195).

Boman strenuously argues against any significant commonality between Hebrew thought and that of the other ancient Near Eastern cultures. For instance, he would take issue with the claim of significant similarities between the biblical creation story and Babylonian Epic of Gilgamesh. Many scholars claim the significant dependence of the biblical writers of the flood narrative upon this earlier Babylonian story. Boman would likely stress the dramatic differences between the two tales.

Barr effectively demolished any claim by Boman of scientific objectivity, knowledge of or commitment to the science of linguistics. Boman is unmasked by Barr as selective, sloppy, and inconsistent, arguing for an antiquated form of linguistics that scholars in the field no longer take seriously. Barr's argument was so rhetorically effective that in virtually no time (a year or two) Boman and a few other scholars were discredited and disowned. My only evidence for that is the rapidity with which they fell out of print, and the paucity of mention or consideration that followed.

Why then is Boman not merely an annoying fly or a speck of dust on the academic windshield, to be flicked off without a thought? Why do I believe Boman ought not be lost and forgotten?

First, one must see Boman as part of a larger intellectual movement. I will now attempt to contextualize the Norwegian scholar.

• The Larger Linguistic Context •

Boman was in good company when he claimed that individual cultures had an identifiable *Geist* and that one might locate that *Geist* in the particularities of its language.

Boman borrowed heavily from a school of linguistics known as "linguistic relativism," "linguistic determinism," or "the Sapir-Whorf hypothesis." The theory proposed that language shapes cognition and perception, that you cannot truly think of anything unless you first have a word or phrase for it. For instance, the lack of a distinct formal and informal second person or even plural and singular in the English language, all flattened out to "you," perhaps has had a flattening effect on the way we regard these social divisions. Likewise, something for which you have many words, will exist for you in many more dimensions. Witness the almost mythical account of all the words for snow among the Inuit.[2] (There is in fact no real evidence for this that I have been able to locate, although everyone seems to be aware of it, believe it, and use it as an illustration of one thing or another.)

The idea is stated that the language makes relative each individual culture, shaping its own world—thus linguistic relativism. The Linguistic Relativists never claimed that there were no univer-

---

[2]However, Geoffrey Pullum writes in an article entitled "The Great Eskimo Vocabulary Hoax" (1990): "What a pity the story is unredeemed piffle . . . an embarrassing saga of scholarly sloppiness and popular eagerness to embrace exotic facts about other people's language without seeing the evidence" (28). Pullum goes on to observe that for the Inuit language there are actually only four words representing snow: snow on the ground, falling snow, drifting snow, and a snow drift. In Greenland there are two: snow in the air and snow on the ground. Even in English there are multiple words for frozen precipitation: snow, sleet, hail, slush, blizzard, etc.

sals in language. For example, certain kinds of color perception are limited by the neurobiology of the human person. Kluckhohn has observed that

> Language is physics, biology, and culture . . . limiting conditions and forwardings provided by the constancies of physics and biology. . . .
> All languages have vowels. In all languages an utterance can begin with a consonant. . . . Form-classes are universal . . . all languages have some metaphorically transferred meanings.
> (Kluckhohn 1961, 895 and 896)

Whatever universal features in language there might be, the truly important features were those that made each culture and each culture's language distinct. The language in a sense determined the way a culture would develop, its institutions, kinship relations, conception of God, everything; thus linguistic determinism. Steiner quotes Sapir, who notes that

> The fact of the matter is that the "real world" is to a large extent unconsciously built up on the language habits of the group. No two languages are ever sufficiently similar to be considered as representing the same social reality. The worlds in which different societies live are distinct worlds, not merely the same world with different labels attached. (Steiner 1978, 143)

Steiner himself goes on to observe that "languages generate different social forms, those forms further divide languages" (Steiner 1978, 143).

• The Response to Sapir-Whorf and Boman •

The Sapir-Whorf Hypothesis, Linguistic Relativism, immediately faced serious opposition from others within the community of professional linguists. There were those—Noam Chomsky of MIT most prominent among them—who claimed that the essential components of language, the deep structure, were hardwired into the brain. Such language components had little to do with culture, and the cultural distinctives one notes when comparing language with language are trivial variations on a single, common theme. Language development, it was noted, happens in every community, in every healthy child, in exactly the same manner. Those who teach English (or any other language) to nonnatives regard the peculiarities of the native language as "linguistic interference" in a larger project. Regarding Chomsky and his followers, Steiner notes:

> All languages known and conceivable are, says Noam Chomsky, "cut from the same pattern." . . . Drawing on thirty languages, J. H. Greenberg has listed forty-five fundamental grammatical relations which underlie all systems of human speech and which organize an essentially unitary picture of reality.
>
> (Steiner 1978, 147)

But Steiner goes on to observe:

> Could it be that the theory whereby transformational rules map semantically interpreted "deep structures" into phonetically interpreted "surface structures" is a meta-mathematical idealization of great elegance and logical reach, but not a picture of natural language?   (Steiner 1978, 151)

So the Chomskeyan response to Sapir-Whorf was the rejection and trivialization of all that the linguistic relativist would consider important, the distinctive data that would distinguish one culture from another. There was, it was claimed, no necessary connection between perception and the ability to put that perception into words. One has only to observe that there are many distinctively human though wordless activities—music and art, for instance. The existence of purely human, nonlinguistic activity undercuts the thesis of *linguistic* determinism.

Further, although there may be no distinctive words for an experience in one language, a combination of words can adequately compensate for the lack. For example, one may note the ways skiers describe in English the variations of snow cover, or all the words borrowed from other areas of perception to describe the subtleties of wine.

In summary, the *linguistic universalist* claims that those features that all languages hold in common are the most significant features. The *linguistic relativist* looks to the particulars, what makes languages different from each other, and says *they* are the most important features. The first (linguistic universalism) is the scientific model where the observer stands apart from the observed object. In the second (linguistic determinism), the observer reports an experience from the inside. The scientist looks for universals that are common to many cultures, seeking the underlying structures or principles that hold them together. The linguistic relativist embraces the difference, the particularities, the individual features that set things apart.

There arises here an unusual parallel. What we have produced in this discussion is an almost exact reflection of Boman's Hebrew-Greek dichotomy, only now among the linguists themselves. The Linguistic Universalists are the Greeks. The Linguistic Relativists represent the Hebrew way of thinking.

How might we explain this surprising juxtaposition? I suggest that Boman and Barr reflect a larger division within the academic community, and when they speak of ancient Israel or of Hebrew Grammar, they are speaking—at least in part—about themselves.

If that is the case, the reasons for arguing one position or the other are not evidential but ideological, that is, the commitment to either a universalist or a relativist understanding of grammar precedes and influences the collection and assemblage of evidence. This is likewise true for Boman and, as we shall see, also for Barr.

I willingly concede that Barr effectively, once and for all, demolished Boman's claims of a *scientific* use of linguistics. Boman certainly thought his linguistic arguments were important. But we need not value his linguistic arguments in a similar fashion. I believe his appeal and his influence lay elsewhere. His claim to scientific verification might perhaps be understood as an affectation of his age, not an intrinsic part of his thesis.

• Reflection of the Modern Situation •

I will now explore a contemporary movement of biblical scholarship and look for both parallels and differences between this approach and Boman's. Boman would claim that although the ancient Hebrew world had its own unique identity, it still spoke forcefully to Boman's own world. I claim further that Boman contributes to our current situation, and an examination of Boman will give us insight and suggest much about our behavior and identity in the contemporary academic community.

One issue that has recently gained prominence might be characterized as "ideological criticism." The experimental literary journal *Semeia* recently devoted an issue to the discussion of Fredric Jameson and to issues raised by ideology, politics, and literary criticism as they relate to current developments in biblical criticism (*Semeia* 59 [1992])[3]

One might define ideological criticism as an amalgam of so-called literary methods ranging from deconstruction, reader-response, feminist, structuralist, and formalist. Ideological criticism is characterized by the following features.

The ideological critic recognizes that the act of interpretation is a political act, and those who have controlled the reins of interpretation wield much power in the various institutions. Interpretation requires some particular ideological commitment. There is no such thing as value-free or objective interpretation. Therefore, one should choose one's ideological commitment with care and with attendance to the ethics involved. One chooses a particular reading of a text because it creates conditions of liberation in the contemporary society. Further, ideological criticism accepts or rejects various interpretations by means of the interaction between a given interpretive community and the individuals involved. Such interpretations are in flux; they are subject to change. And yet individuals have a shaping effect upon their communities. There is a recognition of the radical otherness of the biblical text, that the manner in which the Hebrews knew and perceived were in significant ways different than our own.

There is also, however, an attempt, using the *imagination*, to enter into the world of the text, to try to develop a sense of what it must have been like to live there. This emphasis on the imagina-

---

[3]See esp. my article "Up for Grabs: A Tentative Proposal for Ideological Criticism," 35-42.

tion began when the methodologies and assumptions of "New Criticism," birthed by a group of Southern literary critics who interpreted poetry, entered the biblical academy. This methodology for explicating poetry developed among scholars of English literature in various Southern universities. See, for example, W. K. Wimsatt, *The Verbal Icon: Studies in the Meaning of Poetry* (1954); John Crowe Ransom, "Poetry: A Note in Ontology Criticism as Pure Speculation" (1971); R. P. Blackmur, "A Critic's Job of Work" (1971); and Allen Tate, "Literature of Knowledge" (1971).

Certainly Robert Alter, when he published *The Art of Biblical Narrative* (1981), played a key role. Nor should one diminish the impact of Northrup Frye (although not strictly a New Critic), particularly his *Anatomy of Criticism* (1957) and *The Great Code* (1982). Further prominent examples of this crossover methodology would include Edwin Good, *Irony in the Old Testament* (1965), as well as the works of David J. A. Clines (for example, his Word Biblical Commentary on *Job 1–20* [1989]) and Norman Habel (*The Book of Job* [1985]).

After this, many European schools of literary criticism influenced American biblical scholarship, such as the French Structuralists, Deconstructionism, and the Marxists. Borrowing heavily from the New Critics, ideological critics have moved significantly from many of their assumptions, but the overall literary emphasis remained.

There are significant similarities between Boman and ideological critics:

(1) There is both in Boman and in ideological criticism an attempt deliberately to re-create some crucial element, since lost, in the authoritative text. For Boman it was Hebraic thought; for the contemporary political impulse in literary criticism, it is the silenced voice from the margins of society, the voice of the oppressed.

(2) Both Boman and the ideological critics regarded their more senior colleagues (however unjustly) as representatives of an excessively rational and pseudo-objective approach to the biblical material. Robert Bly, strangely enough, has an astute comment on this phenomenon:

Both science and literature advance by means of ritual battles between generations. Eliot invents a new move in the poetic mono-
logue and drives Robert Browning from the field. So-called "New
Criticism" does ritual battle with "historical criticism" during this
time. Later, the leftist criticism of the thirties attacks the New
Criticism, and so on. If each generation embodies some impulse
of warriorhood, literature propels itself forward and escapes stag-
nation. Language bones breaks, but the flow continues.

(Bly 1990, 164)

(3) They affirm the impossibility of objectivity in any rational
inquiry, however inconsistent that might be with their own claims.
By that I mean, there are many objective claims within these
schools, but both schools of thought question the very notion of
scientific objectivity in their theoretical discussions.

(4) They exult in the imaginative, irrational elements in the
human makeup as somehow a source for deeper knowledge. In the
case of Boman, this manifested itself in the Hebrew predilection for
gestalt perception, for motion, dynamism, involvement; in ideological criticism it manifests itself by sensitivity to the "pagan" elements imbedded in the text, by embracing the feminine, or by
highlighting studies on doubt, skepticism, and despair.[4]

I must note, however, significant areas of disagreement between Boman and ideological criticism. Whereas there is an
expressly political impulse in this contemporary version of literary
criticism that is sensitive to the oppression of the poor and powerless, such sensibilities were lacking in Boman. One would more
likely find in him strong antipathy to other cultures. Boman pri-
vileges the perceived Protestant, Western-European-Christian,
"normal" culture. Boman is a spokesperson for his privileged class.

The proponents of ideological criticism possess a greater methodological sophistication than did Boman. Many of the top contem-

---

[4]See, e.g., Phyllis Trible, *Texts of Terror* (1985); and James Crenshaw,
A Whirlpool of Torment (1984); or, more recently, Danna Nolan Fewell and
David M. Gunn, *Gender, Power, and Promise: The Subject of the Bible's First
Story* (1993).

porary literary critics in biblical scholarship have faced and over-come the extraordinary difficulties of maintaining competence in at least two fields. Witness the impact of Mieke Bal on criticism of the Hebrew Bible.[5] Contemporary literary critics paint the differ-ence between humans and the natural world less boldly. For Boman, only primitives, those called pagans or savages, wor-shipped nature. To Boman this indicated their inferiority. Some contemporary literary critics are more open to so-called primitive ideas of the external (nonmental) world, for instance, the Feminist critics and those who are studying the cognate literature.

So what do we learn from a comparison between Boman and these contemporary critics? One can see the importance of the imagination and passion both for the production of biblical litera-ture and its interpretation. Boman's failures point out the impor-tance of methodological precision. One must be self-reflective about strategies and assumptions throughout the interpretive process. More plainly, scholars must know what they are talking about.

Further, there are different ways of looking at things and of interpreting texts, and they cannot all be categorized as right of wrong, better or worse, primitive or modern. We enrich ourselves by trying to see things from other perspectives. Boman speaks on both sides of this issue. On the one hand, he has attempted to intro-duce an alien system into the scholarly discussion; but on the other, he eschewed what he considered to be primitive religious ideas.

• Conclusion •

What have I done here? First, I reviewed this historical moment of intellectual conflict, first Boman, then Barr. Boman makes linguistic claims about Hebrew; Barr refutes them.

Second, since both Boman and Barr claimed conversance with the academic field of linguistics, I surveyed the field concerning

---

[5]See Joebling's article on Bal in *Religious Studies Review* (1991).

these questions: Do cultures and societies bear a *Geist*, and is that *Geist* imbedded in the language?

Third, the divisions among linguists bear some similarity to Boman's Greek-Hebrew antithesis. Both reflect on certain ways to see the world, ways that are often in conflict. I claim that Boman and Barr are participants in a vast debate occurring simultaneously in many fields.

Fourth and finally, I showed how the Boman-Barr controversy affects present Hebrew Bible studies in contemporary literary criticism.

There is however one question that remains to be asked, although I will not answer it in this chapter. I have presented Boman and Barr as opposed. It is as possible to understand them as great allies against a common enemy. There is much agreement between them on many vital issues.

My thesis is, at last, that change comes in the academic world like a tide. Boman and ideological critics represent two waves on that tide. They have the similarities and differences that one might find in two successive waves. And we all, for that matter, are like waves on that tide.

Chapter 3

A Doomed Methodology: The Politics of Wright's *God Who Acts*

Crossing the threshold from one to the other language is fraught with difficulty, to translate literally and thus to lie, or to paraphrase, and in doing so, to blaspheme. —James Crenshaw 1994, 3

This chapter will be easier to follow if you know its structure. It is broken into four distinct though related narratives. After a brief introduction, in the first narrative I try to reproduce Wright's understanding of Hebrew theology. In the second I raise objections to Wright. Then, in the third, I examine the inner significances of these two positions. Finally, I try to draw out some contemporary implications to these readings.

• Introduction •

In the nineteenth century, drawing on the insights of German Idealism, biblical scholars posited a notion of evolutionary progress in the Hebrew religion. It was imagined that starting from the most primitive animistic practices, the Israelites developed towards increasingly more philosophically complex and ethically mature notions of the divine, leading finally to the revelation of God in the person of Jesus Christ. This approach fell under considerable suspicion. How odd it seemed that religious consciousness was moving inexorably towards a climax that corresponded exactly with the dominant religion of Western society and agreed perfectly with the confessional stance of the academics who propounded this schema.

How odd that it reflected perfectly the prevailing philosophical perspective of Western universities.

The evolutionary model of religion has been largely debunked. The notion that religion is simply getting better and better, moving towards some final great unifying burst is now so out of favor that to simply call a notion evolutionary is to dismiss it. In the academy the evolutionary model still operates, not any longer applied to the texts that we examine (such as the Bible) but rather to our evolving self-understanding. It is imagined that when one theory displaces another in the academy, the second theory is always better, that scholars everywhere (with a few minor obscurantists and reactionaries) are marching boldly towards the future, towards more and more accurate models of reality, of how things truly are, or were. There is something characteristically American about the notion of perpetual improvement, and such a notion has penetrated the academy.

People used to think that religion was getting better and better. Now they just think scholarship is getting better and better. This posture necessarily paints the current academic scene as the fruition of centuries of growth and development, and sees in the present age the closest approximation to the truth for which we all have striven. Some have claimed that they see a deterioration in quality and unity from previous scholarship. What these objectors do not understand is that this nostalgia is one of the signs of the presence of such a dominant change in the academy: it is a trailing end. Also, the older period for which some long, reflects a rather insular, homogeneous group of white men that formulated most of theology up until the 1960s. Certainly theology would be more peaceful and stable without the current pluralism—although it may be argued that even in the past it was never stable.

I have chosen to study G. Ernest Wright and specifically his *God Who Acts* published in 1952. Wright provides a good laboratory example of how the concept of evolution functions in both ancient Israel and the Biblical Theology Movement. In his theological writings, Wright actively disputed the evolutionary model of ancient Israel. He argued that there was a single Israelite sensibility that existed from the outset of Israel throughout its history. Wright sees a fundamental commonality to the Israelite response to history throughout all periods of her existence. Others saw such a radical discontinuity that Israel of the tenth century B.C.E. was regarded as completely different from Israel in the sixth century. Wright however argues that Israel did not improve in her essential elements. He writes:

> It is increasingly realized today that the attempt to make of the Old Testament a sourcebook for the evolution of religion from the very primitive to highly advanced concepts, has been made possible only by means of a radical misinterpretation of the literature. (Wright 1950, 12)

Wright however uses this same evolutionary model when he contrasts the imperfect and incomplete in the Israelite religions and beliefs, with its completion in Christ, and more specifically in contemporary, neoorthodox, white, Protestant, male Christianity. So, although he reacts against the older "History of Religions" picture of the development of Israel, Wright provides a new model that still requires a Christological fulfillment, that is, an evolutionary view. Wright provides a field of study that reflects upon a number of different notions of evolution held in tension or opposition.

Wright's overt Christian bias, masked as disinterested archaeology, now embarrasses us, in the way our parents used to when we were with our friends. We are not bothered by the idea of Wright the great archaeologist, but rather by the actual writing of Wright, which no one seems to read anymore. Further, our own sense of evolution will mandate our dismissal of Wright. My informal survey of colleagues pointed out their fundamental discomfort with the very kinds of questions that Wright raises, and his mode of raising them.

Our premature dismissal of Wright is perhaps the most important reason we must more carefully seek to recover Wright's theological ideas. Our very ready tendency to dismiss them, or not to consider them, regarding them as irrelevant, out of vogue, hopelessly old-fashioned, represents a common tendency on the part of new scholars in the academy to murder their intellectual fathers, as a way to assert themselves and establish a place in the structured society of the academic world.

When we in the present age come to question the evolutionary notion in intellectual history (which places the most current methods on the pinnacle), we are forced to reexamine those we have rejected or believe we have "surpassed." Our very disposition to dismiss these older figures points to their importance in our journey to self-understanding. We attend to Wright or lose insight into the subconscious foundations of our own contemporary interpretations.

• The Story from Wright's Perspective •

Although G. Ernest Wright cannot be identified as the founder of the Biblical Theology Movement (which had no single recognizable founder), a scholar of his stature, writing relatively early in the period, had enormous influence, so he demands our attention now. Mauser, in an article on historical criticism notes that

> Perhaps it is fair to say that the movement was spearheaded by G. Ernest Wright, who published in the early 1950s two modestly sized contributions that attracted wide interest and seemed suitable to serve as programmatic statements for a reorientation in biblical studies and a reassessment of their value for other theological disciplines. (Mauser 1991, 99)

Many of the ideas that shaped the movement can be found in Wright, even though he was not the first to say them. Certainly it was the first time those ideas were expressed so clearly.[1]

I chose to read carefully Wright's book *God Who Acts* and to consider how its arguments might or might not be recieved by a contemporary audience. The evolutionary model of the ongoing development of knowledge would insist that later scholarship supplanted Wright and his insights. I wonder though, whether the insights of Wright, timebound as is all scholarship, can be recov-

---

[1]However, James Barr does not even mention Wright in his seminal work *The Semantics of Biblical Language* (1961).

ered in any way? I hope both to use Wright to give me a representative picture of how the biblical academy operated in the early 1950s, and to trace Wright's continuing influence in current theory.

Wright's chief focus in *God Who Acts* lies in his contrast between the biblical religion and what he calls the "pagan" religions of the ancient Near East. Wright sees the key distinction between them in the Hebrew emphasis on the "acts" of God, what God has done on behalf of his people, most particularly in the Exodus, as opposed to other ancient Near Eastern peoples who focus rather on the cycles of nature.

History therefore becomes the ruling idea of his theology. Wright manages to place virtually all of the Hebrew Bible under the umbrella of this "Acts of God" motif. As the Israelites reflected on what God had done, they developed the idea that God had uniquely chosen them, and covenanted to protect them. As they considered their past, they interpreted the stories of their ancestors in terms of this covenant and how it had originated. Further, the prophets reminded the people and called them back to this original commitment. Thus, from a single mighty act, the Exodus, all the important concepts of the Israelite religion were developed.

Although many other aspects of Wright's work have been called into question, this particular insight has remained the consensus in some form for more than forty years. It is difficult to locate its exact origination as an idea within the academy, but certainly Wright's stature not only as a biblical scholar but also as an archaeologist (he was, for example, the founding editor of *The Biblical Archaeologist*), gave his observations great weight. This notion of the historical emphasis of Israelite religion has remained virtually unassailable. In an important work (*History and the Gods*, 1967), Bertil Albrektson attempted to demonstrate that a historical consciousness was present in representative non-Israelite ancient literature, but the importance of this consciousness in other ancient Near Eastern cultures does not compare with its emphasis in the biblical material.

Clearly the archaeological evidence can neither support nor deny the existence of this historical emphasis, because it comes to us in the heavily edited form of a document that has been preserved these many years. If anything, archaeology would work against such a construction. William Dever notes:

> The Hebrew Bible, in contrast to archaeological artifacts, is what I have suggested may properly be termed "a *curated* artifact." That is, it was not long-lost and then rediscovered as a pristine relic, but rather was continually preserved and reused in changing contexts, constantly reworked by both the Jewish and Christian community. (Dever 1991, 199)

When Wright asserts the existence of a historical consciousness in Israel, he thereby claims the uniqueness and superiority of the biblical religion over those of other ancient Near Eastern religions.

Wright's primary assertion of the uniqueness of Israel is based on this Israelite historical consciousness. He insists the Israelite religion is uniquely characterized by its emphasis on history. At the outset, one must develop a distinctive definition of history. Popularly, history has been conceived as "what really happened," but such a construction is virtually impossible to recover and in many cases bears little resemblance to the Israelite style of reportage. There is no reportage that is actually characterized by this objective effort to reproduce the past.

Many historians insist that whatever includes miraculous causation is by definition eliminated from the considerations of history. Such an approach, though defensible on semantic grounds, is irrelevant to our exploration because it begs the question, since we are not dealing with what truly happened, but rather with a certain mode of understanding the past. It is most helpful to understand historical writing as a reflection upon nonrepeatable acts—those that highlight the uniqueness and noncyclical nature of events.

Wright says, "History is the chief medium of revelation. . . . The Bible's estimate of the work of man is thus derivative from its view of the meaningfulness of history" (Wright 1950, 14 and 88). Many have noted the historical identification of YHWH in most important covenantal settings. At the beginning of the decalogue, for instance, God is not introduced as the creator of heaven and earth, but as the God who brought the Israelites out of Egyptian bondage (a historical, that is, nonrepeatable, act).

Further, in the literature, the Hebrew festivals are all linked to historical events in the saving history of the nation. Passover is linked to the Exodus deliverance, Tabernacles to Israel's travels in the wilderness, and so on. One notes that the Israelites consciously debunked cyclical holy times and natural objects in their literature. The sun and the moon, for instance, in Genesis 1, are described as *ma'or*, customarily translated as "lamp." Such luminaries function as signs of the feast days and changes of the season. The priestly writer (at least) is consciously debunking the sacred nature of these objects, rendering them as mere clocks or calendars.

After establishing the importance of the historical conception for Israelite thought, one must then ask whether the remainder of the ancient Near Eastern cultures have no historical consciousness. Albrektson has noted in various accounts of ancient kings both a consciousness of the importance of the political (by definition non-repeatable) realm and the intervention of national gods in that realm. He therefore argues that the Israelite treatment of history is not unique. It is my general impression from published material and papers presented at academic conferences that Albrektson's thesis has not taken hold. Most would regard Israel as *more* histori-cally oriented than Israel's neighbors.

Wright argues (more subtly because even in the 1950s it was questionable to assert a morally superior stance) that the Israelite religion was qualitatively better than that of the other cognate reli-gions. Most obviously he notes that it has endured, whereas the others have not. This, however, begs the question, because it assumes one of the things it sets out to prove: that there is signifi-cant continuity between ancient Israel and its modern children Judaism and Christianity.

More to the point, Wright asserts that Hebrew theology offers hope over pessimism by opening up society to the possibility of change. He asserts that there is no possibility of change in a society that looks towards changeless features of nature for its inspiration. On the other hand, Wright notes, a faith that is defined by the nonrepeatable acts of history is intrinsically more open to the possibilities of societal transformation.

Such a historically conscious people, he argues, do not support a rigid hierarchy, but rather will support social and religious institutions that hold notions of justice and fairness for its citizens. He notes that, historically, pagan religions have resulted in more violent cults and more violent societies. One commonly sees in their practices human sacrifice, and dehumanization of sexuality through its incorporation in cult (see Harrelson 1969).

There is one other consideration, albeit not scholarly in the narrow sense, of which we must be aware. Those of us who teach the Bible or do research in it, for the most part do so because we have an affinity with the material. We usually advocate at least the *significance* of the biblical text. Few of us can claim we are studying this material merely by chance and that it might as well have been any other field of study. As a result, in our teaching and writing many of us have an interest to establish that this particular body of material (that is, the Bible) is worthy of all the special attention it has been afforded. We are therefore predisposed to agree with Wright when he says that Israel is historical, unique in its ancient Near Eastern setting, and superior.

We may however argue with him in some particulars, and perhaps take issue with his sectarian tone. Although Wright strongly disputes the evolutionary view of religious development, he sees Christianity, and particularly Protestant Christianity as the culmination and fullest current expression of the biblical religion, which he sees as consistently held by a significant segment of the Israelites until the advent of the church. At that point, Israel ceased to have importance for Wright in his theological writings.

• The Arguments against Wright's Story •

Many have understood a contrary position: the ancient biblical religion is neither unique nor superior. This is not to say that some other religion *is* unique and superior, but rather that all ancient Near Eastern religions are part of a larger fabric—an expression of their common culture with some particularities, some good, some bad, but having altogether a fundamentally common approach to life.

The following are some ideas that are found in the Bible, and yet are thought more characteristic of a general religious consciousness in the ancient Near East.

(1) Evidence of a violent, temperamental God.[2] There are passages, for example, in which the Israelite God is depicted in frightening, even demonic terms. Examples would include the stories of the Garden of Eden and the Tower of Babel in which deity shows jealousy and resentment when humans encroach upon divine territory; the Flood story wherein God acts rashly and impulsively; Exodus 4 in which God appears in front of Moses and tries to kill him for no apparent reason; Leviticus 10 where God destroys two young priestly apprentices for offering incense in an incorrect manner; 2 Samuel 6 where God kills an unsuspecting Uzzah who tries to prevent the Ark from falling to the ground; 2 Samuel 24 where God orders David to take a census, then punishes him and all Israel for doing so; 2 Kings 2 where in response to a curse from a vain prophet, YHWH sends two bears to tear apart forty-two children; God's activity against Job and against Jeremiah; and some such attitudes are also found in the complaint Psalms.

(2) Acceptance of idols and multiple conceptions of God. There is a clear reference to the acceptability of household idols in some early period of Israelite history. The ancestors, and certain members of the first royal families possessed *Teraphim*, that is, household idols.

(3) Use of mythic forms in Hebrew literature. There are various mythic representations of divine-human encounters. Consider for instance the Psalms that speak of YHWH coming like a storm:

> The voice of the LORD flashes forth flames of fire.
> The voice of the LORD shakes the wilderness; . . .
>
> (Psalm 29:7-8 NRSV)

---

[2]See James Crenshaw, *A Whirlpool of Torment* (1984) for a good discussion of some of these passages.

See also the very old poem in Judges 5 of Israelite victory against the Canaanites:

> LORD, when you went out from Seir,
> > when you marched from the region of Edom,
> the earth trembled,
> > and the heavens poured,
> > the clouds indeed poured water.   (Judges 5:4 NRSV)

There are also poetic passages that compare the word of YHWH to the sun:

> In the heavens he has set a tent for the sun,
> which comes out like a bridegroom from his wedding canopy,
> > and like a strong man runs its course with joy.
> Its rising is from the end of the heavens,
> > and its circuit to the end of them;
> > and nothing is hid from its heat.   (Psalm 19:4c-6 NRSV)

The account of the *bene elohim*—"sons of God"—who mate with human women and produce giants on the earth (Gen. 6:1ff), as well as all the storm imagery connected with the revelation on Mt. Sinai points to a significant identification of YHWH with characteristics of the storm gods. This is in spite of Wright's tortured explanations to the contrary.

(4) Fertility rites and rituals. There is in the Hebrew Bible ample evidence of the kind of magical practices that customarily have been associated with "pagan" societies. Tamar's sacred prostitution brought fertility to the bereft family of Judah (Gen. 38). The stripes on Jacob's sticks magically produced offspring that physically resembled them (Gen. 30). Leah and Rachel compete for the use of the mandrake to assure that they would bear a child for their husband (Gen. 30).

(5) Festival calendars (see Eilberg-Schwartz 1990). Two natural cycles concern the Israelites, the planting cycles and the phases of the moon. They point to a much more refined understanding of the magical powers of these celestial bodies than may be indicated by the polemics of Genesis 1. The Psalms warn of the danger im-

posed by the moon, as expressed, for example, in the phrase "the moon by night" (Ps. 121:6). Further, the Israelite law notes the offering of a scapegoat to a desert demon named Azazel (Lev. 16:8, 10, 26; see Gaster 1962, 325-26, and de Vaux 1965, 508-509). An old but very interesting article by S. R. Driver (1919, 207-208) cites Wellhausen, who suggests that the scapegoat ritual is part of an ancient attitude that the desert is the abode of demons (see Isa. 13:19-22; 34:11-14; Tob. 8:3). The evolutionary perspective claims that this tradition has been "exorcised." But one notes that there are references in Enoch to Azazel, chief of demons banished to the desert (1 Enoch 8:1; 9:6; 10:4-8; see Wright 1950, 91-92).

As a result of the above list, we may conclude that there is a rich relationship between pagan culture and the popular expression of the biblical religion. The biblical text of course represents only the surface of the religious activity that took place in ancient Israel. Illicit contrary positions were systematically suppressed by the writers and editors of the Bible. Popular religious ideas were frequently underrepresented in the canonical form of biblical texts (see Bird 1991).

I differ with Wright in that I am not prepared to argue in favor of the religious position of the dominant tradents (or those who had final say about the Bible) when they claim to have the ultimate right to determine meaning. Therefore, I can at least acknowledge that these other positions have a voice which did not "make the cut," but did however leave their trace. Contrarily, Wright would claim that the Israelites were unique and that the anti-"pagan" elements in Israel most characteristically represented the true Israelite. There are however many qualities in the Israelite religion that are continuous with other ancient Near Eastern cultic, theological, and ethical beliefs.

In terms of Israelite behavior depicted in the Bible, we must admit that there is little evidence of Israelite moral superiority. We might note the concept of *herem*, the Israelite holy war, wherein as a sacred requirement Israelite troops were compelled to commit genocide, destroying all that lived, even innocent noncombatants:

> Now go and attack Amalek, and utterly destroy all that they
> have; do not spare them, but kill both man and woman, child
> and infant, ox and sheep, camel and donkey.
>
> (1 Samuel 15:3 NRSV)

There are certainly many restraints on the full participation in holy
war. There is even some question as to whether it had been carried
out fully in any instance. The fact remains however, that the ideal
of *herem* was favored in the sacred text (see von Rad 1958).
Further, there is ample evidence of social inequity despite the
preaching of the prophets. The treatment of women and foreigners
serves as another example that leads one to question the moral
superiority of Israel.

Elsewhere in the Bible, there are elements of the ancient cos-
mologies that differ markedly from that of Genesis 1 and 2, elements that seem better and more world-affirming than Wright's
portrayal of the Israelite's antinature position. In contemporary
times, it has become increasingly desirable to reestablish the human connection to nature. The connectedness to the forces of life,
the cycles of growth, and the seasons, might replace the idea that
nature is a thing to be mastered rather than a living fabric in
which we all play a role. Therefore, many of the assumptions
modern Western society rejected as superstition in fact might still
have a function in certain instances. Primitive notions of magic
might still prove to be real when we regard them as alternative
avenues of healing and mystical insight.

So many of the things Wright is desperately trying to expunge
from the Hebrew Scriptures are in fact those things that are essential to current notions of an ecologically based spirituality: the
"pagan" notion of a world infused with Spirit, the magical possibilities inherent in the fabric of nature, the unity and commonality
of all personality, whether dead or alive, corporeal or incorporeal,
human or animal. Wright will insist that all traces of such primitive notions have been expunged and defused by the theological
activity of ancient Israelite theologians. In fact, he is correct that
such an effort had been made. But now we need these ideas again,
perhaps even more.

Wright is mistaken, however, in thinking that this effort has been even remotely successful. Much of the Hebrew Bible would agree with Wright, but there are many prominent exceptions or traces. And we must take into consideration that biblical literature in its present form represents most directly the opinions of those who had sufficient power and energy to control and canonize the text. The sides that won gain the right to control the text and its interpretation. There remain numerous traces and even more than traces, of the older ideas that they have not been able to expunge from the Bible. And behind the traces it may be suggested that there lurks a vibrant tradition, hidden, yet still very active within the Hebrew milieu.[3] Wright however goes on to insist that Israel was "not guilty" of such practices.

What are the common techniques for determining which theological construct is most important, most Israelite? Where two opposing features are both present within a given text (as in the opposition between history and nature), it is difficult if not impossible to determine which is more important. One can count the frequency of references in support of a given position and give the award to the one most mentioned. Yet sometimes a subject might not occur because the concept was assumed and natural, not because it was less important; or, the position might not be mentioned because it was so pervasive and yet controversial that it had been suppressed by the final tradents (determiners of the tradition).

Alternatively, some position, such as Wright's idea of the historic nature of biblical faith, might have greatest prominence because it is indeed the most important—but this is circular reasoning. Wright's position claims that Israel identified YHWH as the one who delivered the Israelites from Egyptian bondage in the Exodus introduction to the Decalogue. The Exodus and the Decalogue are, it is presumed, the central pronouncements of the Israelite faith. It

---

[3]Witness the archaeological data as well as some new studies coming out from a sociological perspective, as in Bird's (1991) study of Israelite women's cultic practices.

must necessarily be the most important way that Israel understood YHWH. I argue that we determine a text's importance by virtue of the themes that *we* consider important. In cultic texts, nature, sacral kingship, and mythic themes have great prominence. In historical texts, history is put forward. What does this prove? Nothing.

It is interesting to note that many of Wright's most deeply held beliefs are shared by those who opposed him most strenuously. For instance, both Wright and Gilkey regarded primitive tribal religious practice as contemptible, thankfully replaced by modern, more human-centered understandings of religion, where God is perceived as benevolent and predictable.

Gilkey disagrees with Wright when Wright affirms that early Israel had broken from these primitive practices. Gilkey's counter-position asserts that Israel had never fully broken away from its pagan roots, that only the modern intellectual culture has broken with them. I suggest that this commonality between Israelite conceptions of nature and those of their neighbors might not be so bad. This so-called primitive approach to religion has inherent value, and should exert more influence on our theological constructions.

I am not asking who is correct regarding Wright's story and the contrary position. That would only reduce the whole to a binary opposition, making a complex world into a series of polarities. Rather, we should inquire as to what processes of production are embedded in these two ways of looking at the data. As people interpret these ancient literary and historical texts, they form them into their own coherent narratives or stories: the story of Israel's religious uniqueness and the story of a common ancient Near Eastern *Geist*. Perhaps a more fruitful question to ask would be, Which factors went into each position and how did they produce their distinctive outlooks upon the ancient literature?

• The Underlying Ideology of Wright's Story •

To read Wright is to immerse oneself in both the sensibilities and fears of the fifties. Wright rejected the orthodoxy of his theological fathers. He was clearly drawn towards neoorthodoxy, which sought to restore a sense of revelation to the church. His teacher was William Foxwell Albright, and much of his repositioning is with regard to this man. He more vehemently opposed the old "liberals" who felt that the application of "science" to the interpretation of the biblical text would lead inevitably to the correct solution.

Further, Wright was alternately horrified and fascinated by the Communist menace. Note references to the cold war in *God Who Acts*, for example:

> There is a subtle difference, however, in that while Marcion rejected both paganism and the Old Testament with equal vigor, our modern rejection of paganism, except for the Communist type, is by no means as clear and forthright.   (Wright 1952, 16)

In the modern fight against paganism for Wright, paganism was defined as commitment to a non-Christian idea, (corresponding to what current sociologists of religion might identify as secular humanism).

> Yet biblical hope and pagan comfort are not the same thing. In the present frustration within and without it is futile to speak glibly of peace when there is no peace. . . .

> A new Russian dictionary of 20,000 "foreign" (non-Russian) words and phrases, recently published by the Soviet State Publishing House, defines "religion" as "a fantastic faith in Gods, angels, and spirits . . . a faith without any scientific foundations . . . supported and maintained by the reactionary circles . . . for the subjugation of the working people." The Bible is defined as "a collection of fantastic legends without any scientific support . . . full of dark hints, historical mistakes, and contradictions."
> (Wright 1952, 26 and 117)

Wright's aversion to scientific understanding of religion inevitably associates old-line historical critics with (for him) contemporary Soviet thinkers.

> We are surrounded by myths; we live and breathe them. While the most spectacular is the mythology of communism, those in

which we move are no less important. The spiritual life of the West has maintained itself by a supposedly scientific myth drawn from evolution, the idea of progress, which involves the unverifiable faith that man can be redeemed in history by gradual growth.   (Wright 1952, 122)

Here we see Wright's aversion to communism joining with his aversion to using evolutionary process as a hermeneutical principle.

This fear of the external, of the other, which expressed itself in a fear of Communism as well as in his vitriolic hatred of the non-Israelite ancient religions, caused Wright to close up, and draw to himself those pieces of evidence that pointed to a hermetic Israel, pure from the beginning and remaining pure throughout its existence. Subsequently, Israel passed on this legacy to the church. Wright announces prophetically that God challenges the church to be pure, and to be wary of letting in the contemporary pagan elements.

Wright, in mimicry of the religious tendencies of the people he surveys (those representatives of Israel that he elevates to be the whole) closes himself against outsiders, regarding them with suspicion. It is then understandable why such a scholar would naturally gravitate to those elements of ancient Israel in which he defined himself by contrast to the other nations. The rest follows in course. Those passages that seem to point to a continuity between Israel and its neighbors will either be ignored, reinterpreted, or destroyed.

• The Underlying Ideology
of Those in Opposition to Wright •

Why do many want to stress the Bible's lack of uniqueness? For the most part, contemporary biblical scholars will be predisposed to examine aspects of continuity between the various literatures of the ancient Near East. They respond to questions of Israel's uniqueness with embarrassment, avoidance, or by shifting into a different mode of understanding, one more expressive of their personal religious commitment. "That's a statement of faith," I have heard some say.

I want to examine the various pressures exerted to shape this opposition to Wright's stance. The academic study of the Bible and religion in the United States used to involve almost entirely a white, Protestant, male membership. It now includes other Christian groups as well as other religions, particularly Judaism and Islam, which have now entered into our dialogue. Also, our professional organizations include members of religious studies departments who have (at least institutionally) no connection with a confessional position, and who ask questions that are very different from Wright's concerns.

As a result, it is increasingly more difficult to close in and define *the other* as inherently hostile, without necessarily excluding some of one's own colleagues. A certain amount of openness and willingness for one to exist in an ambiguous common space has become necessary.

The new importance given to issues of pluralism and cross-cultural appreciation will certainly exert pressure on many to shift the direction of their research. In response to the pressure, those in the modern academy seek to expose the provincialism of the biblical text (so as to attack similar tendencies in contemporary society), or to demonstrate the Bible's openness and commonality with other ancient cultures as a means of promoting our own openness to different cultures. A similar process has taken place in feminist theology, where feminist and womanist scholars understand the texts either as examples of a kind of prefeminism, liberating ancient women beyond their cultural limitations, or as indicators of the corrupting nature of patriarchal notions in the Israelite setting. (See Trible 1978 and Felder 1991 for examples.)

Finally, some are motivated to stress the Bible's openness to the spirituality of nature, because they are engaged in a quest for a theology that will be congruent with a concern for ecology. They recognize the danger of nationalism and sectarianism to the preservation of peace on the earth (see McFague 1987).

• Conclusion •

It is impossible to determine the relative weight of the two positions regarding the distinctiveness or continuity of Israelite culture. Rather, one chooses and thereby makes one's own ideological investment in the outcome. As a result, I propose we drop questions such as "Which impulse dominates in Israel?" or "Which one represents a 'pure' expression of the Israelite mentality?" Rather, it is incumbent upon us to examine carefully *both* impulses in Israelite society, one seeking to enclose the society from outside influence, and one seeking to join and combine. Either impulse, unchecked, would necessarily tear a society apart.

Finally, we do well as students of culture to attend most carefully to the voices from our past that embarrass us, that represent the contrary impulse within our own field. We must continue to explore.

Chapter 4

Old Testament Interpretation in the Turbulent 1960s: Barr, Gilkey, and Childs

[In] the aesthetic equation . . . the artist has some internal experience that produces a poem, a painting, a piece of music. Spectators submit themselves to the work, which generates an inner experience for them. But historically it's a very new, not to mention vulgar idea that the spectator's experience should be identical to, or even have anything to do with, the artist's. That idea comes from an overindustrialized society which has learned to distrust magic. —Samuel R. Delany 1976, 183

• Historical Survey •

I have divided this particular historical moment in biblical criticism into three sections: before, during, and after the dominance of the Biblical Theology Movement. I realize that to make such a division begs two very important questions. First, any historical division or periodization is arbitrary and imposed on the material from outside. Second, to characterize various "movements" within biblical criticism is to engage in gross overgeneralizations and caricature.

In my threefold division, the "before" refers to the dominance of liberalism and historical criticism in the first part of the twentieth century. The "during" is the ascendancy of the Biblical Theology Movement in the 1940s and 1950s. The "after," which is my primary focus in this chapter, presents the oppositional work of three biblical scholars in the 1960s who attacked the principles of the movement, and destroyed it.

A brief review of the tenets of the Biblical Theology Movement will be helpful here. The Biblical Theology Movement reacted against the rational liberal nineteenth-century scholarship that disparaged the value of biblical revelation. James Barr notes:

> The atmosphere of the period . . . began with a weariness and a hostility toward the sort of analysis which had dominated biblical study in the source-critical approach: and turning away from this it sought wide synthetic statements which would be valid for the Bible as a whole. . . . [But, he goes on to say,] The biblical theology of the period 1945–1960 was far too much dominated by its reaction against the liberal theology and against the way in which biblical theology behaved in the era of liberal theology.
>
> (Barr 1976, 2)

While acknowledging the modern critical advances of nineteenth- and twentieth-century criticism in the areas of archaeology and history, the Biblical Theology Movement sought to retain a genuine biblical faith. By defending the unity of the Bible and the uniqueness of biblical religion, it employed "revelation through history" as the single unifying principle, asserting that the center of the biblical text was found in God's historical acts (Barr 1961, 5).[1]

This admittedly theological assertion was not defended on dogmatic grounds, but rather (it was claimed) from a critical evaluation of the text and archaeological evidence.

The Biblical Theology Movement contended that important elements of the Bible (its unity and its center in historical revelation) had not been readily apparent to competing schools of scholars because those other scholars did not think "Hebraically." Therefore they had not ascertained the uniquely Hebraic elements in both the Hebrew Bible and the New Testament. Note Barr's comments on the rhetoric of this contrast:

> When objection is made to some theological assertion on the grounds of rationality, it is replied that the supposed rationality

---

[1]See Barr 1966, 16, for further discussion of the search for a center of biblical theology in "the acts of God in history."

is not pure truth, but only one historically given mode of
thought, namely the Hellenic. Given another such mode, namely
the Hebraic, it can be seen that the objections no longer exist. . . .
Thus it is possible to argue that the Hebrew-Greek thought
contrast serves as the historical-cultural projection of a particular
ideal in theological interpretation.   (Barr 1966, 40)

Hebraic thinking (they said) was process oriented, not static; verbal
rather than visual; historical rather than cyclical; dealing in concrete rather than abstract propositions.

The Biblical Theology Movement reacted against more fashion-
able philosophical approaches in both theology and biblical criticism by endeavoring to return to the truly "biblical." One must
both think Hebraically and interpret biblical texts from a Hebraic
perspective. The movement claimed to have rediscovered the way
the biblical writers in the earlier faith communities approached
their material and construed their world. "Its idea is that the interpretation of the Bible must be 'from within' rather than 'from without' " (Barr 1966, 40).

By castigating Greek thought processes and privileging the Hebraic, these writers saw "Athens" as the symbol of all that was negative and deadening in modern academic endeavors. The so-called
Greek philosophical effort to dissect objects in passive scientific
detachment demanded no involvement and no commitment.

In 1961 two works were published that directly attacked the
Biblical Theology Movement. They were *The Semantics of Biblical
Language* by James Barr, a full-length book; and an article by Langdon Gilkey appearing in the *Journal of Religion*, entitled "Cosmology, Ontology, and the Travail of Biblical Language."[2] Their arguments were so effective and persuasive, that within a few years,
the Biblical Theology Movement was rendered powerless. Childs
notes that

In the history of biblical scholarship, certain books have made a
notable contribution by initiating a new approach to old material,

---

[2]Barr subsequently published a number of related books, most notably
Old and New in Interpretation (1966).

such as Gunkel's *Shopfung und Chaos*. Other books have contribut-
ed equally by bringing to an end a phase of research, such as
Schweitzer's *The Quest of the Historical Jesus*. James Barr's book
clearly falls in the latter category. (Childs 1961, 374)

Evidence of the Biblical Theology Movement's decline is found
in their publishing history. For instance, other than the requisite reviews that appeared in 1962 and 1963, arguments against Barr's
and Gilkey's thesis virtually ceased early in that decade. Following
the reviews, the only major scholarly works that I have been able
to locate that substantially interact with the issues raised by Barr's
Semantics of Biblical Language are those written by David Hill, John
F. A. Sawyer, Arvid K. Tangberg, and Paul Ronald Wells. The first
two marshal defenses of the "word-study" approach of the *Theological Dictionary of the New Testament* edited by Kittel, attempting
to incorporate most of Barr's criticisms of that multivolume work.
The third is a reevaluation and confirmation of Barr's linguistic
approach. The final work (Wells) constitutes a conservative critique
of Barr's "liberalism."

At the same time, interest in and work in the Biblical Theology
movement steadily declined. Brevard Child's *Biblical Theology in
Crisis* (1970) signaled the final stage in the dismantling of the Biblical Theology Movement, although the Movement's effects still ling-
er. There are two continuing legacies of the Movement assumed by
most commentators (as long as they are not examined too closely).
They are:

(1) Ancient Israel had a historically based religion, while the
surrounding religions were based on the forces and cycles of
nature.

(2) The Israelite religion is ethical and monotheistic, while the
surrounding religions are polytheistic and wildly immoral.

• Ideology and the Displacement of Biblical Theology •

In a recent article about W. F. Albright, Burke Long states:

I believe that it is time to begin constructing accounts of biblical
studies not so much as histories of great ideas, methodologies, or progress in accumulating reified truths, but as historical

inquiries into ideas mediated through ideologically charged social processes.   (Long 1993, 44)

Long implies that members of the biblical establishment regard themselves as guardians of a body of truths, which we build upon as foundational. Although these truths are *about* events in history, they are *themselves* timeless truths. For instance, it is considered a truth that the documentary hypothesis describes an actual process that took place in the ancient past, resulting in the first five books of the Bible. This "fact," is a timeless truth, "discovered" by Wellhausen and others, and "guarded" by the biblical academy.

Long suggests a different approach to interpreting the ancient texts and understanding the processes of their interpretation. First, Long would see the texts as a product of (as he calls them) "ideologically charged social processes," so that textual production would be understood as caused by individuals of a particular economic class, nationality, race, and gender. This ideological location, Long states, is significantly responsible for the production of this ancient literature. For instance, it is significant whether the ancient Israelite poet was an upper-class Israelite in Solomon's court or an itinerant sage in premonarchic Israel.

Long's second point asserts that *contemporary* theories of the production of this ancient literature also are caused by situations (processes) of economic class, nationality, race, and gender. It is therefore significant that, for instance, Julius Wellhausen came from German middle-class stock.

Long's point is often lost because of two competing understandings of ideology. Ideology is often defined as a "false consciousness," that which deceives both the interpreting subject and the audience. To call an argument ideological then would be to accuse it of dishonesty, concealing oppressive impulses under the guise of rational argument. The other definition sees ideology as the necessary fictive world we all must create in order to make sense out of our existence. Both of these definitions must be held in tension. Understood in this way, ideological activity is both necessary and desirable (see Penchansky 1980, chap. 1). Spivak defines ideology as follows:

> Ideology in action is what a group takes to be natural and self-evident, that of which the group, as a group, must deny any historical sedimentation. (Spivak 1988, 118)

Any ideological idea could be equally understood under either the first or second definition. One or the other definition is usually suppressed by most interpreters when they use the word. Someone else's ideology is false consciousness. One's own is of course simply common sense.

• Ideological Activity of the Biblical Theology Movement •

> . . . for there is no supercultural observation platform to which we might repair. —Richard Rorty (1991, 212-13)

Key critics of the Biblical Theology Movement, Barr, Gilkey, and Childs, accused this movement of engaging in deceptive ideological activity, that is, false consciousness. Their analysis breaks into two related issues. According to Barr, Childs, and Gilkey, the movement is guilty of (1) a pious theological agenda concealed under their putative academic concerns, and (2) self-contradiction, that is, that many of the key claims of the Biblical Theology Movement are in direct opposition to each other, and thus cancel themselves out.

The ideology of the Biblical Theology movement is American Protestant Christianity. The proponents of Biblical Theology are trying on the one hand to recover the Bible from the critics who, the Biblical Theologians claimed, had atomized and thus destroyed the Scripture's effectiveness. On the other hand, the scholars in the Biblical Theology Movement distanced themselves from the fundamentalists who had turned away from the discoveries and insights of the modern academic method. Gilkey paints a picture of the Biblical Theological Movement in which

> We are thus not asking [in the Biblical Theology schema] merely the historical question about what the Hebrews believed or said

> God did—that is a question for the scholar of the history of religions, Semitic branch. Rather, we are asking the systematic question, that is, we are seeking to state in faith what *we* believe God actually did. (Gilkey 1961, 198)

And their claim of the uniqueness of Israel was an argument designed to support the superiority of their own religion. Brevard Childs observes,

> One can hardly avoid the impression that the concentration on the elements of demonstrable distinctiveness [of Israel, when compared to other nations] was basically a form of *modern apologetic* [emphasis added], which like the medieval proofs for the existence of God, maintains its validity only among those who had already assumed its truth. (Childs 1970, 77)

Biblical Theology collapsed under the weight of these, its own internal contradictions.

These critics accused the Biblical Theologians of undermining their own arguments by putting forth or using exactly contrary principles at the same time. Gilkey claims that their words mean nothing at all. He notes that although the biblical theologians claim to have demonstrated the historical activity of God, they in fact remain subject to modern scientific assumptions about miracles:

> Do we have any idea at all to what sort of deed or communication [in their discussions of and definition of miracles] these analogies refer? Or are they just serious-sounding, biblical-sounding, and theological-sounding words to which we can, if pressed, assign no meaning? . . . Thus they repudiate all the concrete elements that in the biblical account made the event itself unique and so gave content to their theological concept of a special divine deed. . . .
>
> The modern assumption of the world order has stripped bare our view of the biblical history of all the divine deeds observable on the surface of history, as our modern humanitarian ethical view has stripped the biblical God of most of his mystery and offensiveness. (Gilkey 1961, 199 and 196)

Gilkey's major point was that biblical theologians—the attack was again directed toward Wright and Anderson—had tried "to have their cake and eat it too." They used biblical and orthodox language to speak of divine activity in history, but at the same time continued to speak of the same events in purely naturalistic terms: "Thus they repudiate all the concrete elements that in the biblical account made their event itself unique and so gave content to their theological concept of a special divine deed" (Gilkey 1961, 199). Gilkey's criticism was particularly painful because it raised the fundamental question of whether the recourse of the biblical theologians to history had in fact succeeded at all in solving the old crux between the Conservatives and the Liberals.

Eilberg-Schwartz, anthropologist and rabbi, writing in 1994 quotes Wright and von Rad while commenting upon this issue:

> Along with this fundamental rupture in religious consciousness appeared an equally significant development in moral insight. This is particularly evident when Israelite religion is compared with that of the Canaanites. "The sexual emphasis of Canaanite religion was certainly extreme and at its worst could only have appealed to the baser aspects of man. Religion as commonly practiced in Canaan, therefore, must have been a rather sordid and degrading business, when judged by our standards, and so, it seems, it appeared to religious circles of Israel" (Wright). When scholarship exposes the mythological and polytheistic context out of which Israelite religion emerged, "one cannot marvel enough at the power which made it possible for Israel to break away from this world of ideas and speak about the relationship of God to the world in quite a different way" (von Rad). [Eilberg-Schwartz goes on to comment] Quotations such as these could be readily multiplied. What they show is how often the desire to situate Israelite religion against the background of the ancient Near East has served a *defensive posturing and evolutionary agenda.*
> (Eilberg-Schwartz 1990, 14; emphasis added)

Barr points out that the linguistic claims of the Biblical Theology Movement are ill-founded and do not represent their true purpose (see chapter 2, above). Both Barr and Gilkey claim that the

Biblical Theology Movement misuses and distorts science for theological ends. One notes an interesting relationship between Barr and Gilkey. Gilkey claims that the theological assertions of the Biblical Theology Movement do not adequately coincide with their decidedly modern cosmology: that is, they claim they have isolated the genuine moment in which God has acted in history. In fact what they have done is completely reduce the activity of God to an interpretation regarding their faith in events, events which are otherwise entirely explainable in a naturalistic sense. Barr, on the other hand, exposed the *scientific* claims of the Biblical Theology Movement as ill-founded, based on naive and outmoded notions of linguistics. Their claims, seemingly scientific, are in fact theological.

So Gilkey asserts that the Biblical Theology Movement is *more scientific* than it claims. Barr asserts that the Biblical Theological Movement is *less modern* and less scientific than it claims. For Gilkey, theology conceals modern, scientific ontology, while for Barr scientific arguments conceal outmoded theological positions. Both Barr and Gilkey claim that the Biblical Theology Movement misuses and distorts science for theological ends.

• Ideological Activity Found within the Critics of the Movement •

The fusion of horizons [is] not simply the formation of one horizon. . . . Every encounter . . . involves the experience of tension between the text and the present, the hermeneutic task consists in not covering up this tension by attempting a naive assimilation but consciously bringing it out.
—Hans George Gadamer (1975, 273)

Long, however, claims that *all* scholarly activity stems from "ideologically charged social processes." I have presented the work of these critics, Barr, Gilkey, and Childs, as if they engage in dispassionate analysis, that they are not advocates for any position that interferes with their objectivity. In fact, I would claim rather that these critics of the Biblical Theology Movement are equally ideological in their enterprise, but this is not necessarily a bad thing.

• Ideological Activity of Gilkey and Childs •

It is relatively easy to uncover the ideological efforts of Langdon Gilkey and Brevard Childs. Each for his own purpose is attacking the Biblical Theology Movement so that he might advance his own proposal which would then displace this dominant biblical position. We must locate Gilkey in the swirl of controversy following the advance of the "Death of God" theology. Gilkey was arguing from the sense of betrayal that he felt at the failure of the Biblical Theology Movement to sustain him against the early onslaught of the "God-is-dead" theologians. Gilkey wanted to preserve the possibility of "God-talk" against (what came to be called) Deconstructionist attacks. Gilkey observes:

> I was intrigued and yet horrified by his [Thomas Altizer's] abandonment of the word "God" and the very cogent reasons he gave for this new move in theology. . . . Altizer . . . at dinner also declared that God was now thoroughly dead. . . . I did not agree with this new secular theology at all; my cumulative experience of twenty-five years had assured me in countless ways of the reality, the power, and the grace of God.   (Gilkey 1988, 23)

Gilkey is working first of all from his disappointment with the Biblical Theology Movement, a personal disappointment, in that this movement did not give him adequate ammunition to combat what he felt were the overly secularized tendencies within his own field of systematic theology. He needed a basis for maintaining God-talk within an increasingly secularizing and chaotic world. Further, Gilkey notes:

> I knew I needed to find some deeper theological grounding for my continuing allegiance to the Christian symbols. . . . How did I know, how could I know, in the secular world we all inhabited that the divine we spoke of and witnessed to was *real*? . . . Could I also feel and then articulate an *answer* to these arguments, a defense of the religious discourse they found now so meaningless?   (Gilkey 1988, 24)

This was exactly what the Biblical Theology Movement had insisted they were able to do. Without jettisoning scientific and scholarly reasoning, the Biblical Theology Movement claimed to have uncovered a way to speak about the historical acts of God that took place in the human sphere, and thus allow modern thinkers to speak about such activity of God in a more expansive way than liberalism allowed. For Gilkey, they had failed to make their case. Although he dates his concern with the "God-is-dead" movement to 1963 (two years after his "Ontology" article) the concern with developing an adequate basis for God-language is present in his earlier work. In "Ontology" he is trying to clear the underbrush for his own proposal which is essentially an effort to sacralize the secular thinking of the modern era. I am not in a position to comment upon or criticize his efforts here, but it is clear Gilkey finds the Biblical Theology Movement unsatisfactory and needs to eliminate it from consideration in order to establish his own way.

Whereas Gilkey ultimately finds transcendence in the religious sensibilities of the secular world, Brevard Childs, a biblical scholar, tries to find transcendence in the text. The Biblical Theology Movement "privileged" a particular intellectual moment in the history of Hebrew thought which the biblical theologians characterized as "Hebraic," and they sought to interpret all of the biblical text, Old *and* New Testaments from this perspective. Childs and his followers, however, privileged the particular textual activity of the Christian interpretive communities throughout their history. Childs did not mean to imply that there were not other communities interpreting the text as well, but he argued that the Christian was (at least) one community through whose eyes the text may speak authoritatively. Childs does this not by thinking "Hebraically," but by examining the Bible's use in successive Christian communities. Childs claims:

> One of the persistently weak points of the Biblical Theology Movement was its failure to take the biblical text seriously in its *canonical* form. It accepted uncritically the liberal hermeneutical

presupposition that one came to the biblical text from the vantage point outside of the text.   (Childs 1970, 102; emphasis added)

• Ideological Activity of Barr •

Barr is more difficult to locate ideologically. He states no clear agenda regarding with what he would replace the Biblical Theology Movement. Some significant comments about Barr's location, however, can be made at this point.

The very absence of an obvious advocacy on the part of Barr is a significant feature of his work. Barr is highly selective in the material he chooses to dissect and analyze. One cannot help but notice that Barr's most important, incisive, and influential works are directed specifically and pointedly at those scholars who seek to establish a biblical basis for transcendence, by which Barr means the objective activity of God either in history or in sacred text.

Barr has published at least four books that relate in some way to the claims of the Biblical Theology Movement: *Semantics of Biblical Language* (1961), *Old and New in Interpretation* (1966), *Biblical Words for Time* (1969), and *The Garden of Eden and the Hope of Immortality* (1992). He has published two books on fundamentalism: *Fundamentalism* (1977) and *Beyond Fundamentalism* (1984). He has even written a response to Brevard Childs's attempt to recover some of the theological claims of the Biblical Theology Movement: *Holy Scripture, Canon, and Authority* (1983). This list of course does not include his many articles and more general books, some of which impinge upon these subjects.

In fact, Barr is a veritable one-person "truth patrol," seeking out and destroying those methods that make unfounded transcendent, religious, theological claims. He seeks to debunk the various modern efforts to establish divine activity in the biblical realm. Barr has little patience with facile claims that the Bible somehow self-authenticates. He seeks out those schools of criticism that make precarious claims, ill-founded and/or dishonest. He has never met a metaphysician that he liked.

Barr's powerful, emotion-laden rhetorical activity is also an indication of ideologically charged interpretation. He employs rhetorical devices such as judicious and purposive assemblage of evidence, use of the riveting story and emotion-laden words, rhetorically charged words and phrases such as "merely," or "of course we all know" (or some such variation), in an elegance of formulation. Many have noted Barr's strong and forceful argumentation that sometimes goes beyond the bounds of simple logical refutation. He can be insulting and mocking when it suits him. Note his words in a footnote to *The Semantics of Biblical Language*:

> What has been called "biblical theology" is often an evasion of exact study on both the exegetical and the dogmatic sides and does harm to both . . . an attempt which is absurd when coming as it sometimes does from writers who not only boldly transgress modern linguistic methods but *do not even know what they are.*
> (Barr 1961, 280; emphasis added)

Note the following rhetorically charged descriptions Barr gives concerning his opponents:

> All this may be interesting and intelligent material, and I have no intention of criticizing it here; but it goes far beyond the elucidation. . . .
>
> There is indeed a quite considerable number of articles in which different sections are headed "linguistic" and "theological"; the dangers of such a practice are obvious and serious. . . .
>
> I mention all this not in order to depreciate Oepke's own opinions. . . . It is a Bible-mysticism, at times sublime, which however has nothing to do with sound scholarship."
> (Barr 1961, 229, 230, and 231)

Note how Barr tends to praise slightly and then eliminate out-of-hand.

It would seem that Barr's chief rhetorical devices are repetition and calumny. R. B. Y. Scott (1962, 516) observes Barr's rhetorical abuse of the Biblical Theology Movement:

> [Barr characterizes them] from a strictly linguistic standpoint as "absurd," "exaggerated," "irresponsible," "misleading," "very naive," "perverse," and even "comical." (Scott 1962, 516)[3]

Robert Gordis (1979, 195) describes Barr's style as "arguing by epithet."

Finally, Barr, tongue planted firmly in his cheek, announces his own ideological agenda:

> The secret assumption behind it all, the spoor I should follow would be . . . the Scottish tradition of commonsense philosophy. . . . For all those who believe that books should be read for their assumptions rather than for their arguments, I make a free gift of this information. (Barr 1968, 385)

This rather subtle comment conceals some astounding assumptions. Barr is thereby asserting that one's arguments should be a function of facts that are unaffected by ideological "spoors"; arguments are or at least should be objective and ideologically free.

I have two conclusions from these observations of Barr's interpretive activity. First, Barr claims forcefully that his scholarship is ideologically free. Second, he seeks to expose all scholarly efforts that he deems to be tainted with various forms of advocacy, whether on the right or on the left. The second point has to do with transcendence. It certainly could be coincidental that so much of Barr's work debunks transcendent claims, but I doubt it. There are two possibilities here. Either Barr does not believe any transcendent event is possible in the temporal world and so will refute any so-called scientific or historical claims to the contrary; or perhaps more likely Barr has such a high regard for transcendence that he will not tolerate its inadequate defenders. My careful reading of Barr and my personal interviews and correspondence with him have not yielded an adjudication to this dilemma that I have in locating the ideology of this venerable scholar.

---

[3]See also L. Derousseaux (1976) 39.

• Overview of Ideological Activity •

I draw a few preliminary generalizations following the observations of Barr, Childs, and Gilkey, before moving on to other related issues.

(1) All interpretive activity is ideological. The issue is not *whether* ideology is being used, but *which* ideology is being used, and who benefits from that ideology. The critics of Biblical Theology saw an improperly formulated attempt to assert ideological hegemony by the church. And then they exercised their own ideological legerdemain upon the working of the biblical text.

(2) The demonstration or proof of advocacy does not eliminate an interpretive observation out of hand. If all interpretation is some form of advocacy, then an ideological interpretation is not necessarily a wrong interpretation.

(3) Self-contradiction within an interpretive system does not automatically eliminate that system from serious consideration. As I have demonstrated elsewhere (Penchansky 1989, 24-25), it is out of the conflicts within a system and between systems that the creative energies flow.

(4) The passage of the Biblical Theology Movement from serious consideration within the academy to near irrelevancy is an example of one ideology replacing another. This is not unfortunate or heinous; it is simply what we do.

In this chapter it remains for us to identify in more detail the inner dynamics of this historic moment in biblical criticism, understood in terms of its ideology.

• Binary Oppositions •

A frequently used device in the establishment of ideological dominance within a field of interpretation is the creation of opposing pairs of concepts which then define the examined object under the rubric of this binary. The most obvious example, the famous Greek/Hebrew split, was central to the Biblical Theology Movement's understanding of the Scriptures. Many other binary oppositions can be identified within the whole range of debate during this period. Implied in all of these divisions are notions of good/bad, inside/outside, self/other; that is, one of the pairs is considered (in almost all cases) to be the "right" one, to be identified with the interpreter. Jameson makes the following important observation:

> The least interesting thing to do with an interpretive quarrel is to decide that one of them is right and the other one is wrong. Maybe there are circumstances where you have to do that; there might be political reasons for trying to do such a thing. Interpretation has nothing to do with correct or incorrect readings, because that has to do more with the establishment of the text . . . then we are talking about the establishment of the primary text itself. . . . No interpretive act of that kind can be completely wrong. Something in the text must have solicited even the most aberrant readings one can imagine.   (Jameson 1992, 233)

Oppositions form "sides" between and within texts and interpretive communities. They declare certain groups and practices "good" and others "bad," dividing peoples into categories of "us" and "them." Jameson claims that all such binaries are highly ideological, and, for Jameson, polar thinking becomes a kind of original sin, the source of all conflict. He says:

> *The true form of evil* here is not the obvious one but maybe the very opposition between good and evil itself. Here is the basic inauguratory opposition which creates the violence and then into which all of these other things can be invested.
> (Jameson 1992, 230; emphasis added)

He continues:

> I . . . feel strongly that one should fight without notions of good and evil in that sense; that is, without anything that validates the self and our people as opposed to their people—that seems to me to be the most pernicious feature of any collective politics.
> (Jameson 1992, 237)

I agree with this sentiment and find Jameson's reasoning compelling. In terms of our analysis, Jameson's assertion will affect us in two ways.

First, I do not seek to determine whether the Biblical Theology Movement is correct or wrong or whether the critics' arguments were well founded. Rather, I seek to understand the "ideologically charged social processes" that both produced the Biblical Theology Movement and led to its downfall.

Second, I will note that most of the arguments made throughout this period took the form of binary oppositions. Specifically "liberal" bifurcations which employ their evolutionary model includes primitive/modern, critical/precritical, and ethical/cultic. The Biblical Theology Movement's bifurcations include Greek/Hebrew, unity/fragmentation of the Bible, and pagan/Israel. The critics of the Biblical Theology Movement imply the following bifurcations: what the Bible means/what the Bible meant (Stendahl 1962), history/theology, and fact/interpretation. Most biblical critics during this period, regardless of their persuasion, employed among others the following bifurcations: science/ideology, general revelation/special revelation, lesson/story, and propositional truth/narrative. The examination of these bifurcations (I would claim) leads directly to their "ideologically charged social processes."

The Biblical Theology Movement characterized its predecessors as evolutionary in doctrine, who saw religion as developing from primitive and cultic to modern and ethical. Note how the argument is arranged in binary terms. The later, more prophetic movements in Israel, it was claimed, disparaged the cult, displacing *cultic* attitudes with *ethical* requirements.

The Biblical Theology Movement argued that this bifurcation was false, that, in fact, Israel was a consistent unity throughout its history and was always distinguished from its surrounding, cognate cultures. In framing their argument in this way, the Biblical Theology Movement employed the bifurcation of their teachers and colleagues: both the so-called liberal Historical Critics *and* the Biblical Theology Movement strongly distinguished themselves from paganism. Paganism was bad, and all that was truly Israelite (defined in varying ways) was good. The Biblical Theology Movement disagreed with their predecessors when they asserted that Israel had *never* been pagan, whereas the classical nineteenth- and early twentieth-century critics pictured Israel as gradually developing out of a pagan mode. Further, the Biblical Theology Movement saw that Israel, having resisted the incursions of one alien expression of opposition, *paganism*, had to face and resist another, *Hellenism*. Whereas the earlier scholars identified Helle- nism with a high and glorious advance in the state of religious and philosophical thought, the Biblical Theology Movement rejected such notions and insisted that at heart Israel, and then the New Testament church, had always maintained a distinctive Hebraic world view. But both nineteenth-century liberals and the Biblical Theology Movement accepted the *same* bifurcation.

The critics of the Biblical Theology Movement rejected its bifur- cations as hopelessly anachronistic and inadequate. But their argu- ments were characteristically binary as well. These critics regarded themselves as careful textual scientists whose examination of the evidence remained entirely ideology-free. In *their* bifurcation, they see scientific scholarship in opposition to ideological manipulation of the evidence. The chief sin of the Biblical Theology Movement, according to its critics, was their imposition of a pious agenda upon their scholarly analysis of the Bible. As their critics saw it, the *ideology* of the Biblical Theology Movement is their *theology*.

We have seen three distinct ways in which the chief partici- pants in this period employ binary oppositions to advance their arguments. For the liberal Historical Critics, it is primarily their distinction between primitive and modern understandings of reli- gion. For the Biblical Theology Movement it is the Greek/Hebrew division, and for the Critics it is their distinction between those who bring ideology to their analysis and those who do not.

More interesting however are those instances where they all share the same bifurcated view of reality. This leads me to con- clude that at a deeper structural level the three groups I have iden- tified are representations of the same basic High Modernist im- pulse within the academy.

There are two chief areas of agreement, and I will here suggest some lines of inquiry about them both. It remains for my last chapter to draw them out more completely.

The first agreement is in fact their division of the scholarly world into two camps, those who are scientific scholars, and those who are—Dare I mention it?!—theologians. Although the critics of the Biblical Theology Movement hold this position most prominently, all parties to this dispute share it, that is, they all see themselves as more scientifically true to the text than their adversaries.

The members of the Biblical Theology Movement also regarded themselves as critical scientists, distinguishing themselves from the earlier less-scientific approaches. This explains their strong emphasis on linguistics and archaeology, "harder" sciences than straight literary or theological analysis. But this scientific claim of the Biblical Theology Movement led to its downfall. They painted with a broad brush, and made many less-than-careful generalizations. The Critics were able to effectively disprove their scientific claims, and thereby eliminate from consideration any of their wider theological claims.

The other universal bifurcation concerned the distinction between pagan and Israelite, which remains fundamental to our notions of the unique contribution of the Bible to Western culture. However they apply the notion *temporally*, the liberals, the Biblical Theology Movement, and their Critics all regarded paganism as bad, and themselves as decidedly not pagan.

In spite of their surface disagreements, the liberals, the Biblical Theology Movement, and the Critics Barr, Childs, and Gilkey, agree on a deeper structural level. This is demonstrated by their shared bifurcations. What exactly is it about which they agree? I suggest the following.

(1) Perhaps what we observe is biblical criticism in the act of defining its membership against outsiders, identified as either the church, secular society, or non-Christian scholars. I understand such shared ideological perspective as an effort to preserve their world against all these attacks.

(2) The underlying bifurcations might represent an attempt to impose Apollonarian order on what was in many of its manifestations a Dionysian, disorderly religion.

If we accept Jameson's contention that the act of binary opposition is a source of distortion and violence, it becomes incumbent upon us to devise new ways of shaping our discourse. My suggestions regarding how to do this will be the concern of my final chapter.

Chapter 5

The Politics of Biblical Theology's Resurgence

Romanticism, which has helped to fill some dull blanks with love and knowledge, had not yet penetrated the times with its leaven and entered into everybody's food; it was fermenting still as a distinguishable vigorous enthusiasm in certain long-haired German artists at Rome, and the youth of other nations who worked or idled near them were sometimes caught in the spreading movement.
——George Eliot, *Middlemarch* (1871–1872) 272

• Imagination and the Unity of the Text in the Biblical Theology Movement •

In this chapter I examine the governing principles that produced the controversy in the Biblical Theology Movement, and then how those same principles, though differently configured, express themselves in the contemporary postmodern situation in biblical criticism. What is interesting is that although the key motives that generated both the movement and its opponents still are present, there is no movement that one can point to that represents these two principles in exactly the same combination— that is, there is no Biblical Theology Movement redivivus.

The first governing principle is the importance of the imagination in the processes of interpretation. This relates to the possibility/impossibility of being scientific in those processes. The second governing principle is the issue of the unity/disunity of the biblical text.

• Imagination •

In the Biblical Theology Movement, clearly the role of the imagination takes a central place. Much of what the Biblical Theologians wrote is a particular expression of the larger Romantic movement, which in turn had reacted strongly against the nineteenth-century historicism of much scholarship in that era. At least that is the account of the Romantic period that dominates academic discourse in the middle to late twentieth century in North America. The Romantic movement arose in the nineteenth century (with roots in the eighteenth) in reaction to the rise of positivism which had swept over the western European intellectual world beginning in the time of the Renaissance and the Enlightenment. The Biblical Theology Movement only expressed this wider impulse in the field of biblical criticism. In this case, the Positivists were represented by those who interpreted the Bible claiming the possibility of scientific precision, the historical critics.

The problem is, with the Biblical Theology Movement as with Romanticism as a whole, the accusations against the biblical Positivists were largely made up of caricatures. A careful examination of the so-called Positivists would demonstrate that the best of them were highly imaginative and creative thinkers in their own era, and they knew it. Hermann Gunkel was one who was closely identified with the earlier stages of historical criticism. His *Legends of Genesis* (1901) is a surprisingly sensitive literary reading of these ancient tales. One begins to realize that the entire portrayal of nineteenth- and twentieth-century Positivists is in fact a propagandistic attack by the Biblical Theology Movement against the current ruling party in biblical criticism at the time.

There were among the biblical critics that were *not* part of the Biblical Theology Movement in that era some highly imaginative and creative figures, who, although not trained in literary criticism, made some wonderfully sensitive literary readings of the Hebrew Bible. Another figure who comes to mind is Gerhard von Rad, who, although occasionally tiresome in his endless quest for sources (his *Genesis* commentary for the Old Testament Library, for instance), can (as in some passages in his *Old Testament Theology*) create a very persuasive narrative world, one that affected and continues to affect many readers of the Hebrew Bible to this day.

The Biblical Theology Movement's portrayal of those against whom they defined themselves was caricature and propaganda designed to make the Movement look good. Further along the same observation, we may note that the Biblical Theologians' claim to stress the imagination was somewhat deceptive as well. As we have seen with Wright and Boman, much of the warrant for their assertions comes from pseudoscientific argument; at least they employ science in the service of pseudoscience. By this I refer to Boman's use of linguistics (see above, chap. 2) and Wright's use of archaeology (see above, chap. 3). But in spite of this disingenuousness, it still remains an important observation that the Biblical Theology Movement stressed imagination over dispassionate scientific observation in the processes of interpretation. This is the first principle characteristic of the movement.

• Unity of the Biblical Text •

The second principle regards the unity of the text. The proponents of the Biblical Theology Movement (I have argued) were centrally concerned with the ideology of the unified text. On this, they believed, hinged their entire metaphysical underpinnings. Their understanding of God and their understanding of the sacred text depended upon their affirmation that the text was unified and came from a single divine, and in the case of certain individual books from a single human, hand. They had much invested in this assertion, and would argue strenuously, using any conceivable warrant available to them, that the text (in an objective sense!) was unified, that in all of its parts it said the same thing.

This phenomenon—the assertion of the Biblical Theology Movement that the text was unified—informs us of many things. I do not believe that what is most important about the Biblical Theology Movement is their method for arriving at conclusions, because this method borrows directly from the prevailing ethos of their age, that is, the scientific approach. In spite of their rampant Romanticism, they still appeal to science to determine their approaches to the ancient material. Rather, more important than their method are the stands they take for the imagination and also for the unity of the text.

When examining these two principles, we find that the opponents of the Biblical Theology Movement (whom I have isolated as James Barr, Langdon Gilkey, and Brevard Childs) take the exact opposite positions on both of these principles. On the issue of the role of the imagination in the processes of interpretation, James Barr, for instance, reveals strong skepticism against the sloppy and intuitive conclusions of many in the Biblical Theology Movement, observing that they were entirely too dependent upon their own theological biases in order to determine their conclusions. Gilkey and Childs follow suit. Childs certainly feels that the imagination can retain a proper role in the act of interpretation when it is performed by members of a believing community in the ongoing development of the canon. But for the most part, the opponents to the Biblical Theology Movement directly attribute the biases of Boman, Wright, and the others to their imaginative theological excesses.

And in terms of the unity of the Bible, Barr and Gilkey stand foursquare against the whole notion. In most cases they do not even mention the issue; but where they do, they regard the Bible, as did most of the historical critics of a previous generation, as a multiplex document incapable of harmonization. The historical critics therefore abandoned any effort to take in the Bible as a whole, or even to harmonize an individual book, but rather sought to examine one particular stage in the process of canonical development. When historical critics studied the oral form they called it form criticism. When they analyzed some of the earlier written collections of the material, it was called "redaction criticism" in the New Testament or "tradition criticism" in the Old Testament. Childs studied the processes of interpretation that continued to take place after the moment of the text's fixity—the moment after which readers of the text could only add commentary, but could not change the actual letters and words of the text. This moment is of course a mythical moment, and can never be reliably fixed, except within a range of fifty years or so; and fifty years is an enormous leap of time in the early stages of canonical formation. These canonical critics examine the text as it changes after this moment of fixity.

Others chose to examine the sweep of the process, as a religious text went though many of these stages. Von Rad tried to do that, although he was not entirely successful. He began to lose interest in the processes of the development of the tradition after the moment of textual fixity, although theoretically nothing would necessarily have stopped him at that point in the process. Von Rad is a Protestant for whom the theological events that took place following the fixity of the text were of lesser importance than those things that happened before.

But no historical critic claimed that the text as it presently existed manifested a harmonious whole. Rather they saw it as a long, drawn-out process that went through many hands. And the biblical tradents that made their contribution to the understanding of the text frequently did not agree. And one of the goals of the historical critic was to search for, highlight, and examine the moments where two or more different grand traditions clashed in the actual formation of the text, such as the disjunction between the Yahwist and the Priestly source in the development of the Pentateuch.

In summary, we see the Biblical Theology Movement concerned over two major areas: (1) the role of the imagination and (2) the unity of the biblical text.

The opponents of the biblical Theology Movement denied the importance of the imagination, opting instead for a more scientific, rational approach. Further, they denied the unity of the biblical text, seeing Scripture more as a complex set of differing traditions and theologies created over a vast span of time.

• Imagination and the Unity of the Text in the Postmodern Era •

[First Gentleman]: All choice of words is slang. It marks a class.
[Second Gentleman]: There is correct English. That is not slang.

[First Gentleman]: I beg your pardon. Correct English is the slang of the prigs who write history and essays. And the strongest slang of all is the slang of poets. (George Eliot 1871–1872, 140)

Now we jump to this current, postmodern era, and we find that the concerns are very much the same. I will remind you of my comments at the end of chapter 3 that academic discourse could be understood as a series of waves. In some ways, in general shapes, each wave resembles another, in that there is a succession of crests and troughs of varying intensities, heights, and lengths. And there is certainly a sense, as wise Qoheleth told us many years ago, that "there is nothing new under the sun" (Eccl 1:9). It is not enough however to simply observe these similarities. Rather it remains for us to continue to reflect *in what ways* the concerns of the post-modern era resembles that of a previous time, and *in what ways* they are different. And one of the most notable differences that I observe is that the configurations of these two concerns is dramatically different in respects, although not directly opposite. Opposite would mean that we note two groups, one that emphasized the imagination and the disunity of the text, another that emphasized a scientific (not imaginative) approach while claiming that the text is dramatically unified. We have something like that, but not an exact mirror image.

The two examples of contemporary imaginative approaches to the Bible that I discussed in the earlier chapters were both identified as part of the larger category called "Literary Criticism." Some follow the traditions of "New Criticism," also known as "Narrative Criticism," as exemplified by Robert Alter, David J. A. Clines, and Norman Habel, to give some examples from the study of the Hebrew Bible. They affirm the unity of the text and the importance of the imagination. Their characteristic "close reading" borrows heavily from the imaginative faculties.

The other group that manifests these concerns I have called "Ideological Critics." The Marxists, the Feminists, the Deconstructionists, the Reader-Responsists, and the Formalists influence these approaches as they develop their own close, imaginative reading. But *their* reading, though imaginative, taking the form of a persuasive narrative, is anything but unified. Rather, as did the historical critics, the ideological critic examines the fissures, the cracks in the text, out of which is revealed the substance of textual formation. They uncover the Israelite groups whose ongoing conflicts formed the text as we now have it. The Ideological Critic in contrast to the historical critic, however, is self-consciously literary. By that I mean that the critic takes advantage of most of what is current in literary criticism (as it exists as a collection of methods employed to examine literary, usually not sacred, texts). What results at the end of the process of ideological criticism is a persuasive, highly political *story*. A good example of this may be found in the more recent writings of Danna Fewell and David Gunn, particularly their works *Compromising Redemption* (1990) and *Gender, Power, and Promise* (1993), which self-consciously contain actual retellings of biblical stories, renarratizations. In *Gender, Power, and Promise* they tell the various stories in the cycles of Genesis through 2 Kings as if it were a single story, which they call "the Bible's First Story."

For individuals such as Fewell and Gunn, trained in historical criticism, who know all about the "Documentary Hypothesis," and the "Deuteronomic History," to speak of this amalgam of stories coming from various periods in Israel's history as a single story is truly astounding. But they are not attempting at all to harmonize all of these narratives and various theological positions as if they were a single story. Rather they see this "single" story as a swarming mass of contradictory portrayals and clashing ideas. And, not the least, many of the ideas therein expressed clash with the very specific ideological position taken by the authors Fewell and Gunn.

In *Gender, Power and Promise*, Fewell and Gunn ignore history, or any real reference to the processes by which the text was produced. The politics and ideological subjugation they uncover are within the final form of the text. In spite of the obvious limitations of such an approach, it uncovers some interesting relationships between the disparate parts. It is *not* like Robert Alter and the New Critics, in the willingness of Fewell and Gunn to see disjunctions within the text and not attempt to harmonize them within some *biblical* whole.

In the more recent stages of biblical criticism, the biblical critic had two choices: either use *historical criticism* to undermine the biblical text, showing it to be something other than what it appeared in its final form; or use *literary criticism*, which invariably affirmed the coherence and unity of the biblical material. Fewell and Gunn offer a third way in which they use literary criticism to subvert the final form of the text. Fewell and Gunn are literary in that they formulate their insights in the form of story, and provide sensitive *literary* readings of these ancient texts. They focus upon the examination of *literary* features such as plot, theme, characterization, and structure. They are not anything like those I have characterized as *New* Critics, who affirm the unity of the text both historically (it was written by one human author) or metaphysically (each book was written by one unconflicted divine author). So, both of these groups, the New Critics and the Ideological Critics, agree on issues of imagination but they disagree when they discuss the unity of the text.

Those in the social-science/social-world school of biblical criticism, who tend to affirm neither the unity of the Bible nor the importance of imaginative activity in biblical interpretation, uncover some of the same remarkable tensions and dissonance that is found by the ideological critics. In fact the social science people and the ideological critics have much to say to each other. Note for instance the unpublished address of Gary Phillips from Holy Cross with the unusual title of "Chargoggagoggmanchauggagoggchaubunagungamaugg, or My Dinner with Andre: A Response to Richard Rohrbaugh's 'Social Science and Literary Criticism: What is at Stake'." The title refers to a Nipmuk Indian colloquial expression which is the name also for a major lake in the town of Webster, Massachusetts. This translation, while disputed, is most likely: "You fish them on your side, we fish them on our side, and no one fishes them in the middle" (Phillips 1991, 1-2). Phillips observes:

> Call mine a "metacritical" concern if you like. Regardless how you wish to name it, my experience tells me that until we are clear about what is at stake in our own discourses and the context from which we speak, both methodologically and epochally,

we will be unable to address the question to anyone else. Before we can fish in the middle waters we must first know our respective shoreline, the methods we use to catch, and how deep the water flows beneath us. (Phillips 1991, 8)

I want to conclude this part of the chapter with a discussion of Jon Levenson's book *The Hebrew Bible, the Old Testament, and Historical Criticism* (1993). Levenson is relevant to this discussion because he presents his sensibilities in a similarly fashion to the Biblical Theology Movement. Levenson's location, however (Jewish, postmodern), changes the configuration dramatically from those of the earlier period. Levenson, because he brings up these debunked principles (the unity of the text and the importance of the, in this case, *religious* imagination), provides the most significant challenge to the particular postmodern reading of these issues for which I am arguing in this final chapter (and indeed throughout the book).

Levenson is similar to those in the Biblical Theology Movement in that he affirms the divine origin of the text from a scholarly perspective and he attacks historical criticism. He is different in that he is Jewish. He is also different in that he is postmodern in his criticism. His affirmation of unity provides an alternative reading to the postmodern reading of Fewell and Gunn.

In the beginning of this chapter I established that the two key features in the Biblical Theology Movement relate to issues of textual unity and the use of the imagination. The Biblical Theology Movement affirmed both, while opponents affirmed neither. Now in the postmodern era we have similar issues being discussed, but with different configurations. I am interested in demonstrating how these same issues that loomed so large in the 1950s and 1960s are considered important in this present day. As with that era, I am using representative scholars to demonstrate how the issues function and severally divide. Levenson provides a good source, because on the one hand he sees many of the tendencies of postmodernism in the most negative of terms. He himself is highly suspicious of interpreting the Bible politically. He is also hostile towards historical criticism, which in an effort to get behind the

Bible (he says) loses completely (or nearly so) what the Bible actually produces. Levenson says:

> Having decomposed the Bible into its historically diverse constit-
> uent sources, the practitioners lack the means to do justice to the
> book currently in our possession as a synchronic, systemic entity.
> . . . why we should concentrate on one rather than another. . . .
> Indeed, a historicism afraid to acknowledge normative judge-
> ments about suprahistorical truth eventually deteriorates into his-
> torical relativism and experiences mounting difficulty . . . loss of
> transcendent goal. (Levenson 1993b, xiv)

Instead, Levenson boldly proclaims the unity of the Bible, which he understands in the context of the religious communities that read it. So Levenson's thesis rises and falls upon this notion of unity.

> That is, if the real author is God, it is of no account which human
> vessel he inspired with any given verse . . . what is essential is
> not the *authorship* of the Torah but its *divinity* and its *unity*. . . .
> The exegetical heterodoxy of these medieval rabbis stemmed not
> from theological skepticism but from its opposite.
> (Levenson 1993b, 69)

Interestingly, Levenson's disparagement of the so-called political interpretation, whether of the old-fashioned historical criticism
or the new, more Marxist-oriented liberation theology or Ideological Criticism, is based on their supposed misapprehension of
the wholeness or unity of the Bible when "properly" understood
in a religious context. In this, Levenson is dependent upon none
other than Brevard Childs, who, as we discussed in chapter 4,
sought to replace the piety of the Biblical Theology Movement
with a new notion of the spiritual excellence of the Scriptures
when they are read and understood canonically.

So we have in Levenson a double link to our concerns in the
discussion of the Biblical Theology Movement. First, he affirms the
spiritual and literary unity of the Scriptures, only for him from the
perspective of Judaism rather than Christianity. Second, he depends on Childs for his understanding of how the unity functions,

and carries this concern into a more contemporary (shall we say postmodern?) perspective.

But curiously, Levenson's criticism of both the older as well as the more postmodern historical critics is itself decidedly postmodern, and our interest in Levenson finds a new point of concern here as well. Levenson, who takes such great umbrage toward others who see in the Bible's theological assertions traces of more mundane, secular concerns, himself sees such political/ideological concerns in the critics that he deconstructs. For instance, he comments regarding Walther Eichrodt:

> Our examination of the theology of . . . Eichrodt shows that his anti-Judaic remarks were not incidental to his theological method. They were owing not simply to social prejudice, but to this intention to show that the covenantal religion of ancient Israel is of a piece with Christianity. (Levenson 1993b, 20)

But curiously, Levenson enlists the help of the Christian scholar Brevard Childs in his task. Childs formulated "Canon Criticism" as a response and alternative to "historical criticism," which had dominated the academic study of the Bible for the last two centuries. Historical criticism works to uncover the historical processes by which the various books of the Bible were formed. Childs's Canon Criticism maintains that historically only the "final form of the text" exercises authority in the religious communities that have preserved and read them. Earlier forms or pre-texts are both wholly imaginary (not a single one has ever been found) and largely irrelevant to an understanding of the Bible.

Further, communities of belief read texts, and therefore these faithful readings somehow control the interpretive results. Traditions of reading reside within particular communities and determine how the Scripture is to be read and used. For Childs and Levenson, such controls are (or should be) *determinative for the interpretive possibilities within a given text*. One should not, (they prescribe) read a text *behind* the received text (as do the historical critics), nor should one read a text that runs counter to the received text (so-called *counterreading*, or "the hermeneutics of suspicion"). These controversial readings, dissenting voices against the text, remain intellectually possible to maintain, but have little to do with interpretation in the areas prescribed by canon criticism. You might be speaking of *something*, but it is not what the Hebrew Bible says.

Moreover, although Childs offers an unambiguously Christian reading of the Hebrew Scriptures, Levenson finds him useful because of Childs's assertion that faithful traditions control the parameters of valid interpretation. For Levenson, although the Christian reading of the Hebrew Bible is possible (and indeed necessary for a Christian), the Jewish community has most faithfully maintained the tenor of ancient Israelite concerns. Levenson, however, never explains how interpretations are validated only *from within* various traditions (the Christian and the Jewish), and yet the Jewish for Levenson is somehow *more faithful*, judged presumably from some place outside both Judaism and Christianity, and therefore able to objectively weigh the merits of both.

Levenson has determined in *The Hebrew Bible, the Old Testament and Historical Criticism* to make a space for Jewish interpretation of the Hebrew Scriptures in a world where two alien systems (Christianity and historical criticism) have held sway. Christianity and historical criticism have seemed to oppose each other, but Levenson has demonstrated that while seeking to move in the direction of pure science and objectivity, historical criticism has blatantly served the apologetic interests of Christianity. In fact, the major figures of Old Testament theological reflection in the past century—Julius Wellhausen, Walther Eichrodt, Albrecht Alt, Gerhard von Rad, for example—all interpret from a narrowly Protestant Christian theological bias. Levenson's observations in this regard are persuasive.

Levenson argues that although historical critics opposed so-called pious interpretations, they themselves are in fact governed not by strict science, but rather by their own Protestant Christian bias.

We see here a classic postmodern trope, a dramatic and ironic reversal. Each position at its heart embodies its exact opposite. So historical criticism at its heart puts forth a pious version of Protestant Christianity, while the Biblical Theology Movement claims a scientific basis. Each position contradicts itself at base. It is not that only postmodern positions function in this way. Rather, all positions, examined from a postmodern perspective, evidence this characteristic.

At this point, I must observe something very strange in Levenson's argument. He attacks the historical critics (specifically those mentioned above) because they are excessively biased towards a particular religious ideology and this ideology skews their interpretations to support Protestant constructions of Christianity. But he also attacks historical criticism for failing to acknowledge that only faithful readings are valid readings of the Scriptures. Levenson acknowledges this tension:

> The brunt of my argument to this point is that the results of the historical-critical study of the Hebrew Bible have rather generally been at odds with the underlying method. The *method* is historical and therefore privileges the period of composition at the expense of all later recontextualizations. The *results* have been skewed toward one of those recontextualizations, the Christian Church. (Levenson 1993b, 96)

But Levenson fails to explain how he can criticize the same group both for excessive devotion to objectivity which *fails* to acknowledge the faithful reading, while *at the same time* covertly devoting themselves to a particular faithful reading. Further, he cannot explain why his interested *Jewish* reading of the Scriptures (ably and persuasively put forth by Levenson) is both *objective*, that is, true to what the biblical text actually says, and *faithful*, in that Levenson places himself squarely within the confines of Rabbinic, Halakhic Jewish understandings.

Levenson lumps together as historical critics many who do not in fact subscribe to that methodology. He finds significant continuity between earlier grandfathers of the movement and some contemporary interpreters. There are (as has often been noted) significant differences between biblical criticism in the 1940s and 1950s when compared with the 1990s. Some have even claimed that a paradigm shift has taken place. Levenson correctly notes the shared assumptions between these two eras—such as the assumption that the *processes* by which the Scriptures were shaped are both accessible and relevant to a contemporary interpretation of the text; also, that texts in their present form are *disunified*.

But Levenson unfairly associates contemporary versions of criticism (feminist, ideological, neo-Marxist, or postmodern criticism, for example) with the naive assumptions of a previous era. Few in the list above would claim that a particular stage in the process of interpretation *determines* valid exegesis. For example, if one could work back to the *actual words* of Moses, Jesus, or Isaiah, such critics would not claim that one would be in the presence of an authoritative text. Few today would make such sweeping (and suspect) claims.

So the real issue in Levenson's attack on contemporary modes of criticism concerns the controversy regarding whether the text is unified or dissonant, just as with the Biblical Theology Movement. In his more lucid moments, Levenson acknowledges that the text can be read either way, and it is the harmonizing impulse of the rabbis (as one example) that tie together the disparate parts. But Levenson would further claim that a dissonant reading of the received text is neither *useful* nor *faithful*. But what Levenson masks as his own disinterested scholarship, is in fact a well executed ideological thrust. These three are always connected in Levenson's writings: (1) a claim for the unity of the text with (2) a claim of divine authorship of the text and (3) a support for the most stable members of the Israelite society, their reading as final tradents. This authorized reading coincidentally supports the present-day power structures, whether of society at large, synagogue/church, or academic guild.

Levenson makes a link between divine authorship and a unified, coherent text, and such a link cannot be justified. The religious authority of the text does not depend upon that text being unified and coherent. And to deny the text's coherence (to see conflicting theologies embedded in the text and counter-theologies suppressed by the text but still there) is not to deny the authority of the text. Neoconservatives like Levenson cannot, by fiat, remove those of unlike mind from the guild. Nor may he deny to modern historical and ideological critics the opportunity to speak relevantly and forcefully to the religious communities that revere the Scriptures.

So, although Levenson himself insists that the Scriptures have a center, which claim is decidedly modern, he willingly and skillfully and in a postmodern fashion deconstructs his opponents. He does not however deconstruct himself.

Levenson provides for us a contemporary example of one who argues for the unity of the biblical text as did the Biblical Theology Movement. Further, he argues against the project of the historical critics, both those of the classical period such as Wellhausen, Eichrodt, Gunkel, and von Rad, as well as their more postmodern manifestations, as exemplified by George and Mary Coote and George Pixley. And he does his own criticism in a postmodern fashion.

My other example, Danna Fewell and David Gunn's *Gender, Power, and Promise: The Subject of the Bible's First Story* (1993), interests us for quite different reasons. We must first note that nowhere in Levenson's work is his attack on the historical critics attributed to their lack of imagination, that is, their failure to appreciate or be sufficiently sensitive to the sense or shape of the Hebrew story. This of course was the criticism leveled by the Biblical Theology Movement against the historical critics. Rather, Levenson, taking on the role of nonbiased scientist, claims that he is merely uncovering the objective truth found in the text when properly understood. In this he has more in common with the historical critics than against them. Levenson was not subject to the vagaries of Romanticism, and the accompanying understanding of the Biblical Theology Movement and the (new) literary critics who came after them. Levenson's insistence upon the unity of the text comes from a different, more theological source.

Fewell and Gunn, however, are self-conscious in their "literary" approach. They claim to be recounting "The Bible's First Story." Imagination, particularly the imagination required to fill in the gaps left by the Bible's narrative, figures prominently in Fewell and Gunn's project. In this respect, Fewell and Gunn share a Romantic sensibility with their earlier precursors, among whom are those of the Biblical Theology Movement. Fewell and Gunn seek in their work a careful analysis of the role of sex, gender, and women in the literature of the Bible from Genesis through 2 Kings inclusive, to provide a coherent picture of the whole *as if it were* part of a single story. In this they would *appear* to subscribe to the doctrine one finds in both the Biblical Theology Movement, the (new) literary critics and Levenson himself. However, as we shall see, the notion of literary unity found in Fewell and Gunn is quite different from those notions found in these other works.

Fewell and Gunn go beyond notions of the Documentary Hypothesis or the Deuteronomic History and combine all of the speculated documents J-E, P, and D into a single story, presumably the story of some exilic editor who gathered diverse materials from many sources in order to form his single complex work. In a manner similar to the (new) literary critics, these authors for the most part ignore issues of textual transmission that historical critics see as so centrally important, and rather look for ways the various sources that made up this larger story might be read as a single coherent though complex work.

Everything I have so far said would place Fewell and Gunn clearly in the camp of those who see the text in a unified fashion, those I have mentioned earlier in this chapter. But nothing could be further from the truth. I locate Fewell and Gunn as postmodern critics who practice Ideological Criticism. Previous to this work, they were contributors to and editors of the Westminster/John Knox series "Literary Currents" which published some of the most self-consciously postmodern work that has been done on the Bible.

There are a number of characteristics that set apart Fewell and Gunn in their work from Levenson, the New Critics, and the Biblical Theology Movement. A brief review of the four key aspects of postmodern criticism from chapter 1 will make this clear.

(1) *The presence of contradictions.* Fewell and Gunn acknowledge contradictions in the story they have constructed. Further, they do not seek to smooth over or harmonize these contradictions, as many have done. Whereas others have demonstrated that the contradictions were only apparent, or were relatively unimportant, or were intentional to make some larger ironic point, Fewell and Gunn use the contradictions to bring us to the very heart of the conflicts that produced the biblical text. In most cases, after they

highlight the contradictions they proceed to make these inner textual struggles work for them in illuminating their exegetical project.

(2) *No center.* Although Fewell and Gunn allow that the final product of Genesis through 2 Kings is a single story, they do not allow that this story had one center, or one overriding purpose that overshadowed all of the other possible positions that the various tradents took or may have taken when contributing their part. They do not allow the final editor absolute say as to what aspects of the text were important and central, and which others might have been marginal. Rather, they consciously seek out those aspects of the text that might have been marginalized by the later or the latest tradents, and make those the most important for the project they have set out to do.

They are, for example, especially interested in the roles of the women in the various stories, even women that a cursory reading of the text might overlook. David left ten concubines in his palace when he fled Jerusalem, pursued by his son Absalom. Absalom raped those concubines to assert his own power, and when David returned victorious he never slept with these women again but condemned them to perpetual "widowhood." Fewell and Gunn use the story of these women as their centerpiece for the discussion of the reign of King David.

(3) *All readings are political.* Fewell and Gunn's reading of the text of the Bible is decidedly political. They seek always, even in the most "spiritual" texts to uncover the lines of power that conceal the oppression that existed at the heart of Israelite society, oppression of the poor, the women, the children, and the homosexual. Their work with the legal material in the Pentateuch is especially telling in this regard, where they see discussions of the "jealousy" of YHWH as indicative of the particular way that women were kept in their place in the Israelite family by their jealous husbands.

(4) *Opposition to bifurcation.* Polarities run rife in the Bible. Divisions are constantly being made between the righteous and the unrighteous, the good and the evil, the insider (Israelite) and the outsider (the *goyim*). Fewell and Gunn demonstrate that such divi-

sions are fraught with ambiguities. The insiders (the patriarch Abraham, for instance) constantly betray weakness and hypocrisy, while the outsiders (Rahab the harlot, for instance) reveal a kind of righteousness and spiritual understanding uncharacteristic of the best in Israel. Fewell and Gunn's efforts to rehabilitate Jezebel, queen mother of Israel and proponent of the Ba'al cult, are indicative of their willingness to reverse and completely eradicate the standard divisions by which most have understood the Bible.

So Fewell and Gunn are not to be counted with those who see the Bible as a single, coherent, and unified spiritual whole. Fewell and Gunn are the types of critics against whom Levenson devotes most of his energy. It remains for us to discuss what the work of Fewell and Gunn has to do with the Biblical Theology Movement and the thesis of this book. At this juncture I will establish the points of connection between the Fewell and Gunn (as represented in their *Gender, Power, and Promise*) and the Biblical Theology Movement. I need to draw out more clearly the positions of Fewell and Gunn on the two central axes on which I have spun this chapter: the use of imagination and the unity of the Bible.

Fewell and Gunn, are willing to see such a large portion of the Bible as a single story, and are ready to bracket out the major historical/critical issues that have concerned most scholars of the Hebrew Bible for so many years. They virtually ignore issues such as later editing of earlier texts, duplicate accounts, flawed accounts, and so forth. In spite of that, they do not see the text as a harmonious whole. In fact, the text as they examine it is anything but harmonious. In this they find themselves foursquare in the tradition of the historical critics of the past and do not identify with the previous moment in literary criticism of the Bible that emphasized the harmony of the Bible's disparate parts.

> It's not a question of emancipating truth from every system of power . . . but of detaching the power of truth from the forms of hegemony (social, economic, and cultural) within which it operates at the present time. (Foucault as quoted in Spivak 1988, 45)

But Fewell and Gunn are doing a new thing, one that has scarcely been attempted before. And this new thing carries on the

Romantic tradition in biblical criticism which has stressed the use of the imagination in order to access the impulse (or impulses) behind the biblical text. In this and their previous book *Compromising Redemption*, Fewell and Gunn have self-consciously engaged in storytelling. Others have noted that all interpretation is a kind of retelling of a previously told story, but Fewell and Gunn most skillfully have endeavored to deliberately retell the story from a perspective *that they themselves have chosen!* And their choice of perspective has less to do with the political and religious concerns of the final exilic tradent of the first biblical story, but rather reflects deliberately the political concerns of the two authors Fewell and Gunn. They choose to read the story from the perspective of the women that the text has marginalized, because they want to make of this text, often oppressive, an agent to liberate the institutions of their own society. In addition to recognizing that the text is a political instrument to affect certain realities in ancient Israel, they also recognize that their own job as interpreters of the Bible is political, and is intended to affect the political climate in the worlds they inhabit.

That they do such things comes as no surprise to any reader of this monograph. I have been arguing throughout that all interpretation functions in a similar manner. What is different about their approach, and that of others who engage the text in a similar fashion, is that they are *aware of their activity and politicize without apology*. This is not to say that such interpreters might not be faithful members of their various religious communities, but rather that they recognize that the traditions of their communities are far more fluid than most would care to admit, and that their role as theologians and biblical exegetes is to influence the flow of traditions in the direction of justice.

It now becomes necessary for me to drop the pretense, the role of objective scholar who dispassionately reports on activities in a given textual field. I spoke in chapter 1 of my chosen field of study—in the case of this book, the work of the Biblical Theology Movement and of the figures that opposed them. I have not sought with any great care to conceal my own involvement in the issues raised by this material, or the reasons why these issues loom so large in my own understanding of the task of a biblical theologian. But here in this chapter, the discussion of Levenson and Fewell-Gunn provides an opportunity to present my own advocacy.

Postmodern critics (perhaps when confused with the narrower field of Deconstruction) have often been accused (very skillfully by Levenson) of not being "for" anything. And it is certainly easier to deconstruct someone else's position than it is to put forth one's own. But a method will ultimately fail if it only impresses everyone with its abstract exposition and intimidating use of jargon. A method must also offer persuasive readings of, in this case, actual classical texts. Jon Levenson and Fewell-Gunn are my proxies to express a battle that is taking place even now within the academy of biblical scholars. In one sense it is a very old battle, and one in which neither side will completely eradicate the positions of the other. Nobody starts anything entirely new, but always builds on the legacies of those who came before, either by defining oneself against the previous dominant position, or by carefully building on the insights of one's progenitors. As we learn in the Latin American novel *Bless Me, Ultima*:

> Ay, every generation, every man, is a part of his past. He cannot escape it, but he may reform the old materials, make something new.   (Anaya 1972, 236)

I contend that the Biblical Theology Movement modeled a powerful thrust of the imagination, and there are few who have matched the persuasive stories they wove from the biblical text and out of their own fancy. They created a "Hebrew mind" that did two things. It reflected their own theological concerns, as any retelling must reflect the concerns of the current storyteller. But they also provided a meaningful access to the classical text of the Hebrew Bible, one that was eminently usable by many others.

Unfortunately, Levenson seeks to recapture a previous historical period, one that the Biblical Theology Movement represents, where a unified world and a unified text still seemed possible and desirable. But even Levenson cannot escape this present postmodern moment; and although he opposes its practitioners, he uses postmodern tools against them. But Levenson's thrust is ultimately a neoconservative one, and although I sympathize with some of his aims, such hegemonistic control over interpretation can no longer be achieved, nor should it be. Levenson is wrong to claim that his way (through the reappropriation of a unified text) is the only *faithful* way to appreciate the Bible.

I rather propose that the approach exemplified by Fewell and Gunn offers more possibilities of faithfully bringing the Bible into this present era, which is characterized by the aforementioned postmodern features. It is imaginative. It is historical. It is political. And it is open to the possibilities of creating a society characterized by the just treatment of its weakest members.

Conclusion

Let us revisit King David, whom we first discussed in chapter 1, this time considering his own accomplishments, rather than his rise to power against Saul. It is impossible to draw conclusions about the king without images exactly the opposite readily emerging from the narrative. For instance, if one decides that David was a good and spiritual king, that YHWH approved of David, there arises in one's consciousness the images of David the opportunist, David the schemer and abuser of others, and, finally, David the adulterer and murderer. But when one decides to consider that David might have been a megalomaniacal despot, such conclusions evoke *their* opposites: David dancing before the Ark (mostly a positive image) or David mourning desperately the death of his son Absalom. One can vacillate between these two positions, or many other nuanced understandings of David, but one will never set upon a single understanding of David. Not only is he difficult to pin down, but the narrative as it exists will unpin any attempt. The narrative of David *appears* to be coherent, and to hang together as a single, unitary text, but the more one examines it, the less and less one appears to have the story under control.

All this relates to the present study in the following ways:

Any solution to the understanding of this academic event in history, the passage of the Biblical Theology Movement into something else, immediately suggests some contrary construction of the material. When one concludes that the Biblical Theology Movement was subject to excessive theological and religious overtones, one sees that such an observation remains accurate when applied to any number of other ideological perspectives. The ideology of a particular academic enterprise, I have shown, is completely characteristic of *all* approaches to the Scripture. The figure of David deconstructs himself, and refuses any permanent reconstruction. This is not a *problem* concerning the passage, but rather its strength.

The Bible, in spite of the (new) literary critics and the canon critics, cannot easily be read as a single unitary narrative—and it is not even desirable that the text be so read. One must necessarily maintain an ambivalence about one's statutory conclusions, or one's imaginative reconstructions, regarding Scripture—David, for example, in particular. One must stay ambivalent regarding whether or not David was a good or a bad person. Likewise, one must stay ambivalent regarding whether or not the Biblical Theology Movement in any way advanced the understanding of the Hebrew Scriptures, or whether the biblical theologians were unfairly driven from the scene by specious arguments. This is not a stable ambiguity in which one settles in and accepts the clearly specified and delineated space where one will allow the presence of this tension; it is rather an ambiguity that keeps shifting and refuses to take any recognizable shape.

> Those who believe that they believe in God, but without any passion in their heart, without anguish of mind, without uncertainty, without doubt, without an element of despair even in their consolation, beleive only in the God-Idea, not God Himself.
> (Miguel de Unamuno, *Tragic Sense of Life*, chapter 9)

I make one further parallel between the interpretive considerations regarding David and wider theological concerns. I notice that the ones who attempt to create an exact and stable shape for the David narrative are also those who seek to create a stable shape for their descriptions of God. And God equally—indeed, moreso— resists any attempt at reduction into some stable shape, one that is amenable to human understanding. Such attempts violate the second commandment, that forbids any stable representation of deity. This is not to say that representations are forbidden. They are clearly not forbidden. Rather, none of these representations, whether something in the arts, an individual, or a human institution, is to be confused with the untenable God. The moment one tries to hold one's construal of God, it leaps out, or drops out, or changes shape so that the important piece you thought you were holding becomes residual. Theology is mostly fluid, although a very thick and slow-flowing fluid.

Whereas in the David story the bifurcation came in the tensions within a single individual, in an additional story from the Bible, two individuals move in directions that the interpreter cannot possibly or effectively control. In the struggle between Jacob and Esau, the narrator appears to have skewed the results. Jacob is clever and focused, dedicated to winning and keeping the treasured birthright. Esau, clumsy and ruled by his appetites, gives away that which is most precious. But Jacob won his prize through deceit, even though it was rightly Esau's. He did it two times! And who can resist Esau's plaintive cry, "Bless me, me also, father! . . . Have you not reserved a blessing for me?" (Gen 27:34, 36 NRSV).

So, to the careless reader, these two provide an unambiguous choice between the good and the evil. But a sympathetic reading will yield a Jacob who engages in questionable, downright nefarious activities. And in Esau the reader will find a big, dumb lug, without a hostile bone in his body, quick to forgive and completely forget past wrongs.

This relates to the present work in the following ways:

The choice that occasionally is presented as between good and evil, is often far more complex. Sometimes the good and evil are reversed. I have been careful to say that in some sense the text itself does this. Of course I know that such speech is metaphorical (which is not to say unimportant). I do not mean to imply the existence of a literal personality who exists within the text and reaches out through the words to shape and affect the perception of those who inadvertently read it, in which encounter the readers place themselves under the control of this alien (though benevolent) power. It is metaphorical in that only in this way can I describe an undefinable force that cannot be traced to the whims of the author, which are invisible save in the traces left in this mythical "text." I describe here the ways in which the text "pushes back." I am aware that such language evades many issues and begs many questions. However, it provides a very effective way to separate good from bad readings.

There are at least two ways to describe this process. Neither one provides the whole story. The first way posits not a hypostatized personal entity, but rather certain tendencies embedded in the text, some placed there by the author and some by the social and political context in which it was written. These "tendencies" remain in the ways the literary features (character, plot, setting, and so forth) are employed, and in the juxtaposition of two or more passages so that they comment upon each other. When one reads a text, these tendencies impress themselves upon the reader: the words generate one impression and overrule a number of others.

This does not mean that these tendencies are irresistible. Quite the contrary, rather that in the presence of these tendencies one is pushed into certain interpretive directions. To uncover these tendencies (which might be understood as textual features) is to push the interpretation rhetorically into a certain direction.

Another way of describing the relationship of the text and the interpreter is that one approaches the text with certain ideological agendas. These agendas turn a malleable text to serve a particular ideology. As I have stated before, there ought be no stigma attached to ideology. One interprets with biases, and these biases determine which of many possible interpretations, or even which parts of a particular text, one will listen to. But scarcely anyone claims that the text is infinitely malleable, although it is certainly more malleable than most people think.

• Summary and Overview •

In chapter one I staked out my site, the way a contractor does before erecting a building. My text was selected writings from Boman, Wright, Barr, Gilkey, and Childs. I selected these individuals and their writings because they provided a snapshot of a single, very interesting moment in the history of biblical scholarship. I portrayed the rise and fall of the Biblical Theology Movement. In chapter 1 I also established and described the tools I would use in my examination: my method borrows heavily from literary, postmodern, neo-Marxist, and feminist criticism. Particularly, the works of Fredric Jameson have imprinted this approach. The method (as much as these things need to have a name) is called "Ideological Criticism."

Chapter 2 began my chronological move through the material. Thorlief Boman, though not part of this American trend in scholarship, was one of its precursors. I placed him in the context of a larger controversy in the field of linguistics, which is in turn part of a yet larger controversy in scholarly discourse between the positivists and the romantics. Rather than seek to determine whether Boman or his adversaries was more correct, I saw both sides of the conflict as reflective of a single moment or trend in European and North American intellectual life.

The examination of Wright in chapter 3 continued the analysis of the Biblical Theology Movement. Wright became one of the movement's major spokespersons and an important theoretician. Wright's efforts to establish the absolute uniqueness of the Old Testament when compared to both other ancient Near Eastern cultures as well as later Greek culture established for Wright and his sympathetic readers the superiority of the Christian religion (actually Western European and North American Protestantism) and its accompanying culture. It also applied a cultural critique of certain intellectual trends within the Western universities.

Chapter 4 brings to prominence the positions that arose to counter the Biblical Theology Movement. These representative figures (Barr and the others) accused Wright, Boman, and their allies of being hopelessly biased, religio- and ethnocentric. But Barr and the others also functioned from within the context of their own ideologies. Surprisingly, their ideologies are at root similar to those of the Biblical Theology Movement.

Finally in chapter 5 I demonstrate that these controversies from an earlier era reappear in different forms in more contemporary approaches. Again, I select samples that reflect larger trends, in this case, a work by Danna Fewell and David Gunn, and another by Jon Levenson. They assume opposite positions on issues of postmodern criticism, but both work skillfully within the same postmodern context, acknowledged by Fewell and Gunn, denied by Levenson.

• Importance and Relevance of This Study •

As I was working on this book, when people asked me what I was writing, I found it difficult to explain. My words became excessively complicated, and my focus appeared to be far narrower than I knew it actually was. Although my subject is a relatively brief period within a larger intellectual process, the observations have far-reaching consequences.

1. *Consequences for Biblical Scholarship.* If I may indulge in a final bifurcation, two fundamental approaches to the Bible are described herein, one that depends primarily upon a complex interaction between the biblical text and the imaginative faculties and one that seeks to base conclusions on the weight of accumulated evidence. Although there are complex interweavings and borrowings between the two, individual biblical scholars will usually make one or the other commitment, whether consciously or not. But those who commit to imaginative interpretation frequently cite historical or scientific evidence to support their interpretive conclusions. And those who commit to a historical, pseudoscientific enterprise remain subject to their own imaginative perspectives, which select and shape the evidence.

Biblical scholarship must increasingly acknowledge the imaginative component in interpretive processes—not just in the selection or communication of readings, but in the actual construction of the readings themselves.

2. *Consequences for Theological Reflection.* Ultimately, speech about the Bible in the Jewish and Christian context becomes speech about God; how ancient Israelites construed YHWH and how contemporary theologians and religious communities appropriate that construal. The battle between the Biblical Theology Movement and its opponents is in essence a battle for the Bible, and what is under contention is God godself. There was significant agreement between the combatants about the nature of God, which makes me want to listen all the harder to the voices that virtually all biblical scholars in the 1940s, 1950s, and 1960s wanted to squelch. I want to deconstruct the bifurcation that both sides accepted, between his-

torical and natural religious belief, between pagan and Israelite. Such bifurcation no longer serves to enhance our understanding of the Hebrew Scriptures. Israel might just as well be seen as a full and rich expression of ancient Near Eastern sensibilities than as its antagonist.

> may my heart always be open to little
> birds who are the secrets of living
> whatever they sing is better than to know
> and if men should not hear them men are old.
>   (e. e. cummings, "may my heart always be open to little")

So what are we left with? Clearly, we are left with ambiguity, the failure of any sort of certainty. But the word failure implies that this is a loss. It is not a loss, but rather an opportunity for creative and committed thinking. Ambiguity, and the disappearance of the center need not cause us despair. Rather, embedded in this experience of reading texts is the possibility of shaping texts. We may shape written texts by our strategies of reading, and we may shape living texts, that is, our lives and our social order, by the way we persuasively put forth our readings in the arena of communal understanding.

I recently took a class in Bonsai, the Asian art of shaping small trees. One starts with a shapeless mass of growth, begins to cut away, until a shape gradually emerges, a shape that has the illusion or appearance of a larger tree. When looked upon one way, the Bonsai artist has infinite choices as to how to shape the tree. The artist might make it windswept, or hanging like a cascade, or standing straight up and formal. But one of the things they told us in the class is, "Listen to the tree." The tree has input in the shape it will take. I do not know how this works, but if you ignore the tree you end up with a mess. I am told by sculptors that the same is true with stone. It is probably true with any artistic medium. I suggest it is true with interpreters of the biblical text. One is faced with almost unlimited creative potential in reshaping a biblical text, but unless one "listens to the text," the results are less than pleasing.

may my mind stroll about hungry
and fearless and thirsty and supple
and even if it's sunday may i be wrong
for whenever men are right they are not young.

(e. e. cummings, ibid.)

Postmodern criticism is not the end of all criticism, criticism understood at least partly as the discernment of *quality* within a work, separating out the wheat from the chaff. Criticism remains what it always has been—a creative rereading of texts from the perspective of a particular methodology and a particular ideology. But what has changed is the consciousness regarding the enterprise. Still we will argue history, and still we will argue literary context. But we will be conscious that our arguments are not about objective facts "out there," but rather about our own ideological commitments as they relate to the biblical text.

Postmodern criticism is not the end of commitments. Instead we endeavor to make our commitments judiciously, and to make them according to our developed ethic for justice, for elevating the voiceless to the place where they might be heard.

and may myself do nothing usefully
and love yourself so more than truly
there's never been quite such a fool who could fail
pulling all the sky over him with one smile.

(e. e. cummings, ibid.)

Bibliography
and Reference List

Albrektson, Bertil.
   1967. *History and the Gods*. Lund: Berlingska Boktryckeriet.
Alter, Robert.
   1981. *The Art of Biblical Narrative*. New York: Basic Books.
Anaya, Rudolfo A.
   1972. *Bless Me Ultima*. New York: Warner Books.
Baily, F. G.
   1991. *The Prevalence of Deceit*. New York: Cornell University Press.
Barr, James.
   1961. *The Semantics of Biblical Language*. London: Oxford University
      Press.
   1962. *Biblical Words for Time*. London: SCM Press.
   1966. *Old and New in Interpretation: A Study of the Two Testaments*. Lon-
      don: SCM Press.
   1968. "Common Sense and Biblical Language." *Biblica* 49:377-87.
   1976. "Story and History in Biblical Theology." *Journal of Religion* 56/1
      (1976): 1-17.
   1977. *Fundamentalism*. Philadelphia: Westminster.
   1983. *Holy Scripture, Canon, and Authority*. Philadelphia: Westminster.
   1984. *Beyond Fundamentalism*. Philadelphia: Westminster.
   1992. *The Garden of Eden and the Hope of Immortality*. Minneapolis: For-
      tress Press.
Bird, Phyllis A.
   1991. "Israelite Religion and the Faith of Israel's Daughters: Reflections
      on Gender and Religious Definition." In *The Bible and the Politics of
      Exegesis*, ed. David Jobling, Petty L. Day, and Gerald T. Sheppard,
      97-108. Cleveland: Pilgrim Press.
Blackmur, R. P.
   1971. "A Critic's Job of Work." In *Critical Theory Since Plato*, ed. Hazard
      Adams, 891-904. New York: Harcourt Brace Jovanovich.
Bly, Robert.
   1990. *Iron John. A Book about Men*. New York: Random House.
Bowman, Thorlief.
   1960. *Hebrew Thought Compared with Greek*. Trans. Jules L. Moreau. The
      Library of History and Doctrine. London: SCM Press/Philadelphia:

Westminster Press. Original. *Das hebräische Denken im Vergleich mit dem Griechischen* (2nd ed., 1954).

Brett, Mark G.
1991. *Biblical Criticism in Crisis? The Impact of the Canonical Approach on Old Testament Studies.* Cambridge/New York: Cambridge University Press.

Childs, Brevard.
1961. Review of *The Semantics of Biblical Language. Journal of Biblical Literature* 80 (1961): 374-75.
1970. *Biblical Theology in Crisis.* Philadelphia: Westminster Press.

Clines, David J. A.
1989. *Job 1-20.* Word Biblical Commentary 17. Dallas: Word Books.

Crenshaw, James.
1984. *A Whirlpool of Torment.* Philadelphia: Fortress.
1994. *Trembling at the Threshold of a Biblical Text.* Grand Rapids: Eerdmans.

cummings, e.e.
1959. *selected poems.* New York: Grove Press.

Dasenbrock, Reed Way.
1994. "Taking it Personally: Reading Derrida's Responses." *College English* 56/3 (March 1994): 261-79.

Delany, Samuel R.
1975. *Dhalgren.* New York: Bantam Books.

Derousseaux, L.
1976. "Review of *Semantique du Language Biblique.*" *Melanges de Science Religieuses* 33 (March 1976): 39.

Dever, William G.
1991. "Unresolved Issues in the Early History of Israel: Toward a Synthesis of Archaeological and Textual Reconstructions." In *The Bible and the Politics of Exegesis,* ed. David Jobling, Peggy L. Day, and Gerald T. Sheppard, 195-208. Cleveland: Pilgrim Press.

Driver, S. R.
1919. "Azazel." *Dictionary of the Bible,* ed. James Hastings, 1:207-208. Edinburgh: T.&T. Clark/New York: Charles Scribner's Sons.

Eichrodt, Walther.
1961. *Theology of the Old Testament.* Volume 1. Trans. J. A. Baker. Philadelphia: Westminster Press.

Eilberg-Schwartz, Howard.
1990. *The Savage in Judaism. An Anthropology of Israelite Religion and Ancient Judaism.* Bloomington: Indiana University Press.

Eliot, George (Mary Ann Evans).
1871–1872. *Middlemarch.* Volume 1. Reprint. Boston: Houghton Mifflin, 1908.

Felder, Cain Hope.
1991. *Stony the Road We Trod*. Minneapolis: Fortress.
Fewell, Danna Nolan, and David Miller Gunn.
1990. *Compromising Redemption: Relating Characters in the Book of Ruth*. Louisville: Westminster/John Knox.
1993. *Gender, Power, & Promise. The Subject of the Bible's First Story*. Nashville: Abingdon.
Foucault, Michel.
1977. "Theatrum Philosophicum." Pp. 165-196. In *Language, Counter-Memory, Practice*, ed. Donald F. Bouchard, 165-96. Ithaca NY: Cornell University Press.
Frye, Northrup.
1957. *Anatomy of Criticism*. Princeton NJ: Princeton University Press.
1982. *The Great Code*. New York: Harcourt Brace.
Gadamer, Hans George.
1975. *Truth and Method*. London: Sheed & Ward.
Gaster, Theodor H.
1962. "Azazel." *Interpreter's Dictionary of the Bible* A-D:325-26. New York/Nashville: Abingdon Press.
Gilkey, Langdon B.
1961. "Cosmology, Ontology, and the Travail of Biblical Language." *The Journal of Religion* 41:194-205.
1988. "A Retrospective Glance at My Work." In *The Whirlwind in Culture: Frontiers in Theology*, ed. Donald W. Musser and Joseph L. Price. Bloomington IL: Meyer Stone Books.
Good, Edwin.
1965. *Irony in the Old Testament*. Philadelphia: Westminster Press.
Gordis, Robert.
1979. "On Methodology in Biblical Exegesis." *Jewish Quarterly Review* 61 (October 1979): 195.
Gunkel, Hermann.
1901. *The Legends of Genesis: The Biblical Saga & History*. Reprint. New York: Schocken Books, 1964.
Habel, Norman.
1985. *The Book of Job*. Philadelphia: Westminster Press.
Harrelson, Walter.
1969. *From Fertility Cult to Worship*. Garden City NY: Doubleday.
Herder, Johann Gottfried (1744–1803).
1782–1783. *The Spirit of Hebrew Poetry*. ET by J. Marsh. Burlington: E. Smith, 1833. Original. *Vom Geist der hebräischen Poesie* (1782–1783).
Hill, David.
1967. *Greek Words and Hebrew Meanings: Studies in the Semantics of Soteriological Terms*. Cambridge: Cambridge University Press.

Jameson, Fredric.
    1981. *The Political Unconscious: Narrative as a Socially Symbolic Act.* Ithaca NY: Cornell University Press.
    1991. *Postmodernism, or The Cultural Logic of Late Capitalism.* Durham NC: Duke University Press.
    1992. "A Conversation with Fredric Jameson." *Semeia* 59:227-37.
Joebling, David.
    1991. "Mieke Bal on Biblical Narrative." *Religious Studies Review* 17/1 (January 1991): 1-10.
Kluckhohn, Clyde.
    1961. "Notes on Some Anthropological Aspects of Communication." *American Anthropologist* 63:895-912.
Levenson, Jon.
    1993a. "The Bible: Unexamined Commitments of Criticism. *First Things* 30:24-33.
    1993b. *The Hebrew Bible, The Old Testament, and Historical Criticism.* Louisville: Westminster/John Knox Press.
Long, Burke O.
    1993. "Mythic Trope in the Autobiography of William Foxwell Albright." *Biblical Archaeologist* 56/1 (1993): 36-45.
Mauser, Ulrich.
    1991. "Historical Criticism: Liberator or Foe of Biblical Theology." In *The Promise and Practice of Biblical Theology,* ed. John Reumann. Minneapolis: Fortress Press.
McFague, Sallie.
    1987. *Models of God.* Philadelphia: Fortress Press.
Penchansky, David.
    1990. *The Betrayal of God.* Louisville: Westminster/John Knox Press.
    1992. "Up for Grabs: A Tentative Proposal for Ideological Criticism." In *Semeia* 59, ed. David Joebling (1992): 35-42.
Phillips, Gary A.
    1991. "Chargoggagoggmanchauggagoggchaubunagungamaugg, or My Dinner with Andre: A Response to Richard Rohrbaugh's 'Social Science and Literary Criticism: What Is at Stake'." A paper presented at the Social Sciences and New Testament Interpretation section of the Society of Biblical Literature annual meeting, 22 November.
Pizzato, Mark.
    1992. "Redressing the Chorus." *Journal of Ritual Studies* 6/2 (Summer 1992): 1-25.
Pullum, Geoffrey.
    1990. "The Great Eskimo Vocabulary Hoax." *Linga Franca* 1/1 (June 1990): 28-29.

Ransom, John Crowe.
   1971. "Poetry: A Note in Ontology Criticism as Pure Speculation." In *Critical Theory Since Plato*, ed. Hazard Adams, 870-90. New York: Harcourt Brace Jovanovich.
Rorty, Richard.
   1991. *Objectivism, Relativism, and Truth*. Cambridge: Cambridge University Press.
Sawyer, John F. A.
   1967. "Root-Meanings in Hebrew." *Journal of Semitic Studies* 12 (Spring 1967): 37-50.
Scott, R. B. Y.
   1962. Review of *Semantics of Biblical Language*. *Theology Today* 18 (January 1962): 516.
Smith, Kidder.
   1993. Review of *The Prevalence of Deceit* by F. G. Baily. *Religious Studies Review* 19/1 (January 1993): 46.
Spivak, Gayatri Chakravorty.
   1976. Introduction to *On Grammatology*. Baltimore: Johns Hopkins University Press.
   1988. *In Other Worlds: Essays in Cultural Politics*. New York: Routledge.
Steiner, George.
   1978. "Whorf, Chomsky, and the Student of Literature" (1974). In *On Difficulty and Other Essays*, 137-63. New York: Oxford University Press.
Stendahl, Krister.
   1962. "Biblical Theology, Contemporary." *Interpreter's Dictionary of the Bible* A-D:418-32. New York/Nashville: Abingdon Press.
Tangberg, Arvid K.
   1973. "Linguistics and Theology: An Attempt to Analyze and Evaluate James Barr's Argumentation in *The Semantics of Biblical Language* and *Biblical Words for Time*." *Technical Papers for the Bible Translator* 24/3 (July 1973): 301-308.
Tate, Allen.
   1971. "Literature of Knowledge." In *Critical Theory Since Plato*, ed. Hazard Adams, 927-41. New York: Harcourt Brace Jovanovich.
Tracy, David.
   1990. *Dialogue with the Other: The Inter-Religious Dialogue*. Louvain Theological and Pastoral Monographs 1. Louvain: Peters Press/Grand Rapids MI: Eerdmans, 1990. As quoted in "Hermeneutical Reflections on Two Conversations with Job" by Jean-Pierre Ruiz, p. 7. Unpublished manuscript. 1994.
Trible, Phyllis.
   1978. *God and the Rhetoric of Sexuality*. Philadelphia: Fortress Press.
   1985. *Texts of Terror*. Philadelphia: Fortress Press.

Vaux, Roland de.
1965. *Ancient Israel*. Volume 2. *Religious Institutions*. Paperback reprint in two volumes. New York: McGraw-Hill. Original one-volume ET, 1961.
Rad, Gerhard von.
1962, 1965. *Old Testament Theology*. Volumes 1 and 2. Trans. D. M. G. Stalker. New York: Harper & Row, (1) 1962; (2) 1965.
1972. *Genesis. A Commentary*. Revised edition. Old Testament Library. Philadelphia: Westminster Press, 1972; [1]1961.
1991. *Holy War in Ancient Israel*. Grand Rapids MI: Eerdmans. Original in German, 1958.
Wells, Paul Ronald.
1980. *James Barr and the Bible: Critique of a New Liberalism*. Phillipsburg NJ: Presbyterian and Reformed Publishing Co.
Wimsatt, W. K.
1954. *The Verbal Icon: Studies in the Meaning of Poetry*. Lexington: University Press of Kentucky.
Wright, David P.
1992. "Azazel." *Anchor Bible Dictionary*, ed. David Noel Freedman et al., 1:536-37. New York: Doubleday.
Wright, George Ernest.
1950. *The Old Testament against Its Environment*. London: SCM Press.
1952. *God Who Acts. Biblical Theology as Recital*. Studies in Biblical Theology 8. London: SCM Press, 1952.
Yeats, William Butler.
1967. *Collected Poems*. London: MacMillan.

Index

The Politics of Biblical Theology. A Postmodern Reading.
by David Penchansky.
Studies in American Biblical Hermeneutics 10 (StABH 10).

Mercer University Press, Macon, Georgia 31210-3960.
Isbn 0-86554-462-X. Catalog and wh pick number: MUP/P115.
Text and interior design, composition, and layout by Edd Rowell.
Cover design (StABH series design) by Stephen Hefner.
Camera-ready pages composed on a Gateway 2000
    (via WordPerfect 5.1/5.2) and printed on a LaserMaster 1000.
Text font: (Adobe) Palatino 11/13 and 10/12.
Display font: (Adobe) Palatino 24-, 12-, and 11-point bf.
Printed and bound by Braun-Brumfield Inc., Ann Arbor MI 48106.
    Printed via offset lithography on 60# Natural Smooth paper.
    Perfectbound in 10-pt. cls stock, printed one PMS color
        (Pantone 228C = Rhodamine/Rubine red), and film laminated.
                                                    [March/April 1995]